D1301722

# A History
## with
# GOD

PASTORAL TEXTS AND RESOURCES DIVISION

Alliance for Catholic Education Press
at the University of Notre Dame

# A History with GOD

MARY C. McDONALD

*Blessings,*
*Mary C. McDonald*

ALLIANCE FOR CATHOLIC EDUCATION PRESS
at the University of Notre Dame

Notre Dame, Indiana

Library of Congress Cataloging-in-Publication Data

McDonald, Mary C., 1944-
  A history with God / by Mary C. McDonald.
      p. cm.
  Summary: "A series of reflective and inspirational essays exploring the
author's relationship with God"--Provided by publisher.
  ISBN 978-1-935788-04-1 (hardcover : alk. paper) 1. Meditations. 2. Mc-
Donald, Mary C., 1944-  I. Title.
  BX2182.3.M385 2011
  242--dc22
                         2011010365

# Dedication

My history with God began in family. My ancestors dwell hidden in every cell of my body. I am a conduit of their faith in God, and their faith in the strength of family that now flows in the veins of my children and grandchildren. It is a history with God that we share, and will continue to live out, each in our own way, for generations to come.

*I dedicate this book to my family,*
*a strong and loving chain of human souls, joined for life,*
*that stretches, but never breaks.*

To
my loving husband, Joe McDonald,
my son and daughter-in-law, Matt and Kate McDonald,
my daughter and son-in-law, Christine and Scott Giles,
and my grandchildren,
Emma, Molly, Jack and Annie McDonald,
Nick and Elise Giles

*With all my love*

# Table of Contents

# A History with God in the Journey Home

# Introduction

There are moments in time when reason steps back and wonder takes over. They are those times when you can sense a thread of wisdom that tethers you to the heart of God. They are those times when you step back and say, "Did that really happen?" I experienced such a time while I was on vacation at the beach.

It was almost sunset, my favorite time to walk along the beach. It is like a spiritual experience when the water is so calm and the beach so quiet. As I walked along the Gulf of Mexico, I picked up tiny tar-like balls of oil which had washed up on shore from a major off-shore oil spill and put them in a paper cup. I thought I'd take them home to my grandchildren. Perhaps they could use them for "Show and Tell" or a Science project. It was a piece of history they might like to see. As I looked down, I saw a bright green object sticking up in the sand. I thought it might be a toy shovel that had been left behind that I could use to scoop up the oil. I leaned down and pulled it up from under the sand. It was a bright green nylon wallet. I thought it might be a child's, but I opened it up and saw that it was packed tightly with credit cards, club memberships, a driver's license, and more money than I thought anyone should carry without a security guard. I had a heartsick feeling for the owner and the panic he might be feeling to have lost his wallet. I walked back to the hotel and spoke to several people at the front desk and in the security office. No one by the name in the wallet was registered at the hotel, and no one wanted to hold the wallet in case the man returned. The man from Atlanta, who owned the wallet, could be anywhere, but he wasn't at home; I called.

I started calling hotels at the beach. After fourteen "no one by that name is registered here" responses, I finally heard an operator say, "I'll connect you."

A man answered in the middle of the first ring. "Are you Mr. Smith?" I asked.

"Yes, yes," he said quickly.

"Did you lose something" I asked.

"My green wallet," he answered. "It had everything in it, everything," he said. He went on to describe everything in the wallet, including the amount of cash.

"I have it," I said.

"Thank God," he whispered. "Thank God."

I gave him the directions to where I was staying and told him I would meet him in the lobby.

My husband and I had just gotten off the elevator when we saw a man who looked like the one in the picture on the license run in the front door, a little boy running with him. I called his name, and he rushed over and said, "I'm Gene."

I handed him the wallet. He hugged me and said, "Thank you. I have been praying all day to St. Paul to find it!"

"St. Paul?" I asked. "Do you mean St. Anthony?"

"St. Anthony!" he exclaimed. "That's right! No wonder I couldn't find it! I should have called my mother to check which saint. She knows all the saints. She has a history with God."

"I am sure the saints take messages for one another," I assured him. "You can thank both saints." I smiled at his faith, but it was his words about his mother that night that tethered my heart to God: "She has a history with God."

We all have a history with God, whether we realize it or not. I have a history with God that I have thought about many times since that night. It is a history that says, "Don't worry; I got your back; it's under control; it will turn out for the best; let Me comfort you; you should listen to Me once in awhile; I forgive you; be patient; I am always with you."

God and I, we have a history together. He was with me in the prayers at emergency rooms, hospital beds, and fearful situations. He and I shared the crises and heartbreaks of family members and friends. I have a history with God in my friendships, at work, in classrooms, in meetings, in decisions, in having the courage to speak and act when silence and inaction are much easier. We have a history, God and I, in the choices I made and in the blessings or crises that followed. I remember the times that I thought that there was no way out of a situation, and God made a way. I remember when I thought all was lost, everything was over, and then God showed me that it was really just the beginning. I remember the times that I said, "Not I, Lord, choose someone else," and then finally did what I knew He was asking. That's part of God's history with me. He gets a little resistance from me every now and then.

I believe that you have a history with God also, especially when you don't feel it. I am sure that you have been through a void and back. That journey you took through fear, illness, death, depression, unemployment, loneliness, divorce, or disaster was with God, whether you realized it or not. You have a history together. So why worry now, when you know that His history with you will last forever? You prayed; He delivered you. You had a problem; He solved it, in His way and His time. You were troubled, and He came to your rescue. You sinned, and He forgave you. You were sad, and He comforted you, lonely and He sent someone into your life. In your suffering, you understood what He went through for you. You have a history, you and God. It is prayer that tethers your heart to God, and love that writes that history. In this book, I share with you my history with God. And through this book, I encourage you to share your history with others. Peace.

*Mary C. McDonald*

# A History
## with
# GOD

# In the family

# A Controversial Blessing

I never thought of Noah as a role model for parents until recently. I was speaking to a group of parents not long ago, listening to their concerns about raising children in such a corrupt and violent world. They felt as if every conversation they had with their children was a warning about a very real possibility of some harm coming to them. It was becoming increasingly more difficult to answer their children's questions without adding to their fears. I understood their concerns. Sometimes we see so much evil around us that we almost forget what trust feels like. How do we know who is right and who is wrong? How do we know who is friend and who is foe? Who let in all the wolves in sheep's clothing? As they spoke, I thought, "Society is not paying attention to its prophets." No, not the prophets of doom, but the prophets of hope. Who is listening to Noah? Who is trusting God? Who is unafraid of the controversy of God's blessing?

It is not easy for parents to be a voice that is counter to a popular way of doing things, counter to what is espoused by society as a more modern approach to thinking. It is not easy to be a parent in a world where terms like "right" and "wrong" are seen as outdated value judgments that have been replaced with subjective rationalizations. It was not easy for Noah, either. He was an ordinary person, a father, trying to raise his family in a world that was about as bad as it gets, corrupt even to the point of incurring God's wrath. But Noah walked with God. God blessed Noah and his family with being change agents in the world. It was a controversial blessing. Noah was instructed by God to lead his family into newness, to leave behind the past and the present, to be set free by the Word of God. Noah risked the controversy of that blessing. God chose him to lead his family to rise to a new level and Noah said "yes." He knew, as the leader of his family, that his purpose was to help his family understand what God had called them to do. His purpose was to guide, direct, and influence them to do something new, something different, to obey God, and to trust the outcome to Him.

Noah, in spite of ridicule and scorn by others, did what he thought was right for his family. He built an Ark. It was a vehicle for God's blessings for his family. Noah was faithful to the mission God gave him of leading his family into new places, in new directions, so that they could fulfill God's covenant, no matter how difficult, no matter how controversial. It could not have been easy. If you have ever taken a family trip, then you know the pitfalls. I can hear it now:

"I don't like boats. Why can't we ride one of the beasts?"

"Why do I have to go when none of my friends are going?"

"Why do the elephants always get to sit next to the window?"

"Why do we always have to be different? Everyone thinks we're crazy."

"Johnny's Dad said it doesn't even look like rain, and he's real smart."

But Noah was faithful to the Word of God. He was a faith-filled father. That was not an easy task for a man who had just invited his entire family, and their pets, on an extended cruise.

> *Noah was faithful to the mission God gave him of leading his family into new places, in new directions, so that they could fulfill God's covenant, no matter how difficult, no matter how controversial.*

Because of Noah's faithfulness, God gave him an insight into a coming disaster. God also told him what to do to avoid the disaster and how he could save his family. Build an Ark.

Whether or not those Noah warned of the impending dangers believed him, he still continued to build. Noah heard God's wake-up call. It is the same call God sends to all of us, even today. It is not a call to doom, but to hope. And that hope lies in listening to God's plan for our families and taking action. It is no easier for us than it was for Noah. We have been called to navigate the Godly relationship of family through the dark waters of a secular society. God's promise to Noah was fulfilled because Noah stuck to his mission to build an Ark, to gather his family together and travel the journey God laid out for them. They entered the boat as a family and came out as heirs to all of God's creation. It is the same promise God gives to us when we follow His plan for our lives.

Perhaps it's time for you to build an Ark, an Ark called "family." Perhaps it's time to draw your family closer to the values you espouse, the virtues you practice, and the Faith you believe. Perhaps it's time to shut out some of the influences in the world that only serve to weaken your resolve to raise your children according to your own God-given spiritual instincts. Perhaps it is time to encourage others by your example and by your invitation to them to share this journey with you, to be family for each other. Perhaps we need to learn that we really are all in this boat together. Perhaps for the sake of the children, all God's children, we should build that Ark together. Regardless of what others say or do, perhaps you should just keep building your family according to God's plan. It is there, in that family, that you will keep alive all that is good. And that family will float in the knowledge that no matter what happens, God keeps His promises.

# A Grandparent's Role

When my fourth grandchild was born, my role was to do what grandparents do: baby-sit. I was in charge of my then two-year-old grandson, Nicholas, until his parents returned from the hospital with his baby sister. My daughter left pages of instructions, but I never had time to read them, so I resorted to a grandparent's right to take the path of least resistance. It is a luxury not afforded to parents. By the time the rest of his family returned home, Nick was a changed man. He had rediscovered the unrestricted use of a pacifier. He kept one in his mouth and a spare in each pocket. He had a bath in the sink, ate frozen yogurt and Cheetos for dinner, and stayed up until ten each night listening to "one more story."

I was confident that his parents would straighten him out as their routine returned, and they did. As for me, I learned what a grandparent's role is really about. Being a grandparent or a great-grandparent of a child in today's society is a particular challenge and a particular delight. My grandchildren don't fool me with their charming theatrics, but I find it entertaining that they try. It didn't take long before they learned that I am a "soft touch," and I confess that on more than one occasion we have become co-conspirators in getting around their parents' rules, like "Finish your dinner, or no dessert." I am delighted that they are always so eager to see me. Their faces light up when I open my front door, and they bound into the house with the expectation of a good time. All that I learned about parenting seems not to apply to grandparents, so I leave the hard part to their parents. Going to Mimi and Pop Pop's house is an adventure in freedom. Yet, I know that grandparents are supposed to be noted for the things they teach their grandchildren. What can I teach my grandchildren that will last longer than a good time? What is my role? What example can I give them that will last a lifetime? I know. I will respect and support the wisdom of their parents.

Parenting has become so complicated today in a society that often seeks to undermine our core values and negate the role of parents as the first teachers of their children. I don't think parents always get the credit they deserve for the strides they are making in raising parenthood to an art form. I remember when mothers had babies, and expectant fathers sat around in smoke-filled waiting rooms with a roll of dimes clutched in one hand, and a list of names and phone numbers in the other. They waited for the results of a very mysterious process to be announced so they could make their phone calls, pass out cigars, and then go back to the business of running the world. Parents today have dismantled the former social order by declaring that parenthood is a joint project. Both mothers and fathers "deliver" their babies and share in the responsibility of childcare in every area from diaper changing to carpools, from cooking to coaching. In a world that often denies the power of family, parents work

> *Parents work together to provide for their children the value system, education and advantages they believe will help their child become a God-centered, successful, happy and productive member of society.*

together to provide for their children the value system, education, and advantages they believe will help their child become a God-centered, successful, happy, and productive member of society. And, as if that wasn't enough, both mothers and fathers go about the business of running the world. They even replaced the cigars with no-smoking signs.

I admire the involvement of parents today, and I am in awe of their energy level. I am, however, puzzled by their inability to appreciate just what an outstanding job of parenting they do. I have spent most of my life with other people's children, and I have seen the fruits of their labors. If there was only one thing I could say to parents today it would be this, "Never doubt your

God-given ability to be a loving, successful, effective parent. You have the ability to be a parent who knows that there are good times and bad, laughter and tears, that an appropriate 'no' is more loving than a million 'yeses,' that right is still right even if nobody else does it, and wrong is still wrong even if everybody else does it, and that God is the source of our strength. When there are times you feel lost, pull over and ask God for directions. He will give you what you need to continue the journey."

All of us grandparents and great grandparents, all of us who have been where you are, all of us who have raised you, all of us are here, first to support you, then to play with your children. We support your rules and your strategies for raising your children, and we want you to know that we understand the challenges you face. When you can let go of the fear of failure, the fear of comparison, the fear of inadequacy, and the fear of imperfection, then you can love joyfully and freely and truly appreciate the God-given gift of parenthood and the wonderful job you are doing. You will also be able to look forward to that blissful time when the pressure is off and you can let your grandchildren eat frozen yogurt and Cheetos for dinner.

# First in Line

Adriana was barely five when I first saw her, and not much over six when I saw her last. She, her mother, and her sister came to this country so that Adriana could receive treatment for her advancing cancer. Her sister was a student where I was Principal. Although Adriana was not able to attend school because of her illness, she would visit often. In spite of her painful treatments, she always had a smile and a way of leaving happiness wherever she went. Adriana would come by my office to visit and wait for her sister to be dismissed for the day. On her "good days" she would dance around the office to my rendition of "This Little Light of Mine." On her "bad days," her mother would bring her in the stroller. She would sit, motionless, except for her eyes that followed my every move as I worked at my desk. After several months, Adriana's conditioned worsened, and she was confined to bed. She was dying. When I visited her, she would draw pictures of hearts and stars and flowers for me. I would bring her pictures of angels and Jesus with the children and tell her that was what heaven looked like. The pictures compensated for my limited Spanish and her limited English. On my last visit, there were no pictures from her, just a faint smile. So I sat by her bed, held her hand and prayed. When it was time for me to leave, she squeezed my hand and said, "I love you." I kissed her good-bye and asked her to tell Jesus I said "Hi." Her mother smiled. She knew Adriana would do just that. Jesus was no stranger to Adriana. Her mother had introduced her to Him a while back.

As I left the room, I thought of the mothers, the parents, who pushed their way to the front of the line, refusing to be held back by the Apostles, so that their children could meet Jesus, to be blessed and accepted by Him. After all, Jesus was a hero to them. Each wanted Him to notice his or her child. I guess it is what would happen today if a hero or a superstar came to town. We might even wait in line hours to get an autograph, a handshake, or a picture. And we'd surely take the children so that they could experience greatness and give them

> *When Jesus called the children to him, He called us all to come, unafraid of great mysteries, just to meet him.*

a memory of a lifetime. Some things never change, except, unfortunately, maybe our heroes. Whom are we introducing to our children today?

Children are teachable, accepting, and unencumbered by unbelief. Faith defines their world. They trust. What children trust the most is learned at home, lessons learned at their mother's knee, words spoken by their father. What we learn as children is our last forgotten memory. Our society often tempts the minds of the children with ungodly values, only to own the souls of the adults they will become. Let us introduce the children to Jesus, and make the worldly heroes of questionable influence the strangers. When Jesus called the children to him, He called us all to come, unafraid of great mysteries, just to meet him. Who better than you, who are responsible for what children learn whatever your role, to push into the line to meet Jesus, regardless of what others think or do to stop you.

The children did not come to Jesus proclaiming their humility, moral superiority, or knowledge. They came, simply trusting the person who brought them. They came, trusting the person who held them up to be blessed by Him. They came because someone who loved them pushed in line so they could meet Jesus. It is still the same. The children still trust us to bring them to the Way, The Truth, and the Life, and we do not rest easy until they are safely in His arms.

# Just Like a Mother

There is a church in Rome, in a city of churches, that is truly unique. It is the oldest church in Rome dedicated to the Blessed Mother. It is not the age or the architecture of Santa Maria in Trastervere, however, that makes it so special to me. It is the 750-year-old mosaic in the apse behind the main altar. The gold-flecked tiles depict the risen Christ on His throne of glory, surrounded by St. Peter and the early Popes who ministered at the church. Seated at His right hand, on the same throne at His side is His mother, Mary, a gold crown on her head. Christ's arm, in a gesture of gratitude and recognition, is around Mary's shoulders.

It is a familiar pose in a family album. It is the gesture of an adult to an adult, of close cooperation, of equality, not of their natures, but of their commitment and realized hopes. I have many pictures with my arm resting around my mother's shoulders taken at those milestone events in my life. I have pictures of my children's arms on my shoulders at graduations, weddings, and family reunions. The gesture always seems to have the same meaning regardless of the event: "Thanks, Mom." I have been in a lot of churches, and I have seen hundreds of pictures of Jesus with His mother. Most depicted an infant, sweet and dependent, nestled in His mother's arms. Some portrayed the agony of a man, dying on a cross while His mother stood watch. Only this one mosaic shows a grown man, acknowledging His mother as a woman of influence and strength. He's thanking her for recognizing that His would be a hard and lonely journey and for understanding His need for her love and support as He carried out His mission of sacrifice and redemption. But then, isn't that just like a mother?

Mary was a woman of insight, patience, and strength. She was a mother who was on an assignment from God to teach her Son God's word and wisdom. She was a woman after

God's own heart, ready to do His will. Like most mothers, she instinctively knew when to ponder and when to act. When her Son was twelve, she reined in His youthful spirit of adventure. When her Son was thirty, she gently but firmly nudged Him into His mission at the wedding feast of Cana. When He was thirty-three, she stood keeping a brave watch at the foot of the cross, determined to remain with Him, encouraging Him by her presence. With His dying breath, Jesus acknowledged her witness of faith as an example for us all. But then, isn't that just like a mother? A mother has the ability to see what lies beyond the present circumstance of her child, no matter how old her child, no matter how long it takes. A mother sees what lies beyond for the newborn, the late-bloomer, or the rebellious teen. A mother sees what lies beyond the indecision and fear of the college-bound, the job seeker, and the one on the brink of a lifetime commitment. A mother keeps a brave watch for her distant child, her addicted child, and her confused child. A mother remains at the side of her dying child, her condemned child, her child in crisis. A mother cradles her child in her love forever, and her heart encourages the gifts of her gift to the world. But then, isn't that just like a mother?

*It is no coincidence that Jesus'
ministry grew out of His family life
and His relationship with His mother.*

It is no coincidence that Jesus' ministry grew out of His family life and His relationship with His mother. It is no coincidence that our own journey does the same. Mary taught us that all things are possible with God. She showed us how to follow the inspirations of grace with a purity of intention. She exemplified a reliance on faith in the face of doubt. She bore misunderstandings, trials, and anguish in humble silence. She linked humanity with divinity and made us aware of Christ's presence within us. She loved faithfully and joyfully. But then, isn't that just like a mother?

# A Parent's Pledge

We are people of ceremony and ritual. Every occasion of transition is cause for celebration. A prescribed formula marks our rite of passage from one status to another. Significant milestones are pronounced by traditional words stating our readiness to take on the new responsibility. Marriage, Baptism, Confirmation, membership initiations, oaths of office, and graduations are all marked by ritual. All the new responsibilities are accounted for, all but one of the most significant—parenthood. A hospital bill is usually the only thing presented to new parents. Becoming a parent needs a ritual. If your parenthood has not been "ritualized" yet, may I suggest the following ritual:

*By the authority vested in me by God, I am pronounced a parent.*

*I give up the right to remain silent. Anything I neglect to say or do that will help my child to become a better person can and will be held against me in the court of heaven.*

*I have the right to say "I love you."*

*I have the right to say "no."*

*I have the right to exercise my judgment as a parent, free from the pressures of my peers and society.*

*I have the right to openly struggle to live faith within the circumstances of our unique family life.*

*I have the right to freely give my child acceptance for who he or she is, not what he or she does.*

*I have the right to simplify our family life by deciding, realistically, what we want to do and what we have time to do.*

*I have the right to put God in the center of my life and the life of my family.*

*I have the responsibility to speak out against the evil that diminishes the value of all life.*

*I have the responsibility to provide my child with the lasting gifts of positive role models, beginning with myself.*

*I will use my God-given parental instincts to guide me in the choices I make for my child. Before each decision, I will pray, weigh the consequences, and seek to bring out the best in all involved.*

*I will respect my child's other parent.*

*I relinquish the right to reach back through the mist of my past to relive in my child what was never lived in me.*

*I relinquish my rigid attachment to a specific outcome, and will live in the wisdom of uncertainty.*

*I will relinquish my authority as a parent only to my child, and only after he or she proves the ability to accept the responsibilities of a mature adult.*

*I am guided by love, supported by prayer, strengthened by faith, and encouraged by God's trust in me, a parent.*

*Having declared this, I will go forth and parent, so help me, God.*

Try it. It could be a ritual that works.

# Parenting: A Gift of Love

One evening, while sorting out my decorations for the approaching holiday season, my entire life flashed before my eyes. It was not a near-death experience that caused this to happen, but a quick glance around that black hole I call an attic. In cartons and on racks and on nails on the wall were countless treasures waiting for future generations to throw out. I guess I'll die before I move again because I'll never live long enough to pack it all. One box, amid the stacks of boxes, did manage to catch my eye. It was a box of "How To" books on raising children.

As I leafed through them I realized how much of the advice contained in these books I didn't take; mostly because I was too busy raising my children to remember what I read. There is one book, however, I have used as a constant source of wisdom. That one is not in the attic, but rather next to my bed.

Whenever parenting seemed a little too difficult and I would grow weary of the struggles, I would meditate on 1 Corinthians 13 and mentally substitute the word "parenting" for the word "love." It would go something like this:

*Parenting* is the gift of Love. Now I will show you the way which surpasses all the others. *Parenting* is patient; even with babies who cry all night or children who want drinks of water or hear "noises" all night or adolescents who want to stay out all night. *Parenting* is kind; it appreciates the efforts of homemade surprises that leave messy kitchens and the beauty in a haircut that didn't quite work out. *Parenting* is not jealous of other children's accomplishments and other parents' successes. *Parenting* is not snobbish, it does not put on airs when you as a parent, or your children, experience success.

*Parenting* is never rude, it respects and cherishes. *Parenting* is not prone to anger but to the strength to hold firm to the values of the family. *Parenting* does not brood over injuries, but recognizes the struggle in the search of each child for independence. *Parenting* does not rejoice in what is wrong but rejoices with truth. There is joy in doing what is right even if you're the only one doing it. There is no limit to a parent's forbearance, to a parent's trust in God, to a parent's hope, and a parent's ability to endure.

There are, in the end, after all of the books about parenting I have read, only three strategies that have lasted: faith, hope and love. And they are all in the same book, the Bible.

# Pictures of a Marriage

There is an Irish proverb that says: "Procrastination is a heavy load." I guess I didn't realize just how heavy a load it is until I tried to move the carton holding our family's photos that are "in transition." You know the ones. You had them developed, enjoyed them, passed them around, and will put them in an album, someday. In the meantime, they reside in a carton. I decided that that someday had come. It was time to update the archives. I started to sort the pictures and pick up where I left off a few years and several special occasions ago. The pictures in our album most likely look like most albums, with one exception; most of the pictures we have from the past few years center on weddings as nieces, nephews, and children of friends were married.

Although the moment was captured for many different couples, there was a certain similarity about the photos. The pictures all captured the joy, promise, and hopefulness of the moment. But these wedding pictures, while reliving the memory of the day, could never begin to tell the story of a marriage or of the Sacrament of Matrimony. Vows are said quickly, but are lived out slowly. The reception of a sacrament and living it out are two different sets of pictures.

Where are the pictures of the commitment of what it takes to transform a promise into a reality? Where are the pictures of the times in a marriage when actions speak louder than words? Where are the pictures when "for better or worse" turns out to be worse, when "in sickness or health" turns out to be sickness, when "for richer or poorer" turns out to be poorer? Where are the pictures when the vows, spoken quickly, were lived out slowly, but they were still lived out? Where are the pictures of the marriage?

Where are the pictures of spouses making time for each other when there was no time? Where are the pictures of the daily triumphs of faithfulness and forgiveness, of trust and patience, of sacrifice and love? Where are the pictures of a marriage when it welcomes the newborn, or the elderly parent, into the family? Where are the pictures that tell the story of the wayward adolescent or the terminally ill child? Where are the pictures of the marriage that show the survival of the routine and the chaos, of separation and familiarity, of the burden of perfection and the frailty of imperfection, of the nightmares and the dreams? How do you photograph short tempers and long memories, compassion and tenderness? The photo opportunities are there in every marriage. We just don't always think to capture the moment of a decision lived out, of a promise kept, of a grace realized. It is in those pictures of the struggles of a commitment of a lifetime that God gives us glimpses of His unconditional love.

Pictures of a wedding are usually placed in an album to admire and reminisce. Pictures of a marriage are placed in the heart to grieve over or to cherish. A marriage is a story of vows said quickly and lived slowly. The Sacrament of Matrimony is a chronicle of the graces received that provide the strength needed to develop stability, endure the hardships, and rejoice

*The Sacrament of Matrimony is a chronicle of the graces received that provide the strength needed to develop stability, endure the hardships, and rejoice in the blessings.*

in the blessings. The sacrament lasts longer than the ceremony and provides the graces needed to live out a commitment that transforms a promise into a reality. How do you take a picture of a sacramental grace? I guess you don't. You just have to be there to experience it. It is these pictures of a marriage that fill our lives. The pictures of the wedding only fill our albums.

It is through the lenses of the heart that we capture what it means for a husband and wife to be one; to be open; to be nourishing and empathetic with each other. It is through the lenses of the soul that we picture the marriage that the Lord builds. It is a marriage that weathers the storms and finds its security and significance from God, not from the world. It is a marriage that is not built overnight, not built on shaky ground. When God is the architect, the marriage is built on a firm foundation of faith. It is built day by day, year by year, season by season, and takes a lifetime to complete. It is always a work in progress. Each year is the most important one, each milestone the most significant. It is a labor of love.

As for my carton filled with pictures, I think I finally found a way not to procrastinate any longer. I'll call it a family tradition to keep our pictures in a "Transitional Carton" and put off filling the album, again. As for the pictures of a marriage, they continue to fill my heart.

# The Arms of God

We live in a world of gurus and experts. There is a plethora of books, an abundance of workshops, articles, and television shows all proclaiming parenting strategies that work. Maybe they do. More often than not, all this external knowledge never becomes wisdom and transformation. If a strategy does fit easily into your daily life, then you never really internalize someone else's solutions. However, you just might continue to cling to the notion that somewhere there is an expert who can save you. You have grown weary of this culture of violence and death. You long for a transformed kingdom on earth. There are times when those who have made peace with the status quo exhaust your vision of what could be, especially the vision about children. That vision is about an awakening of spiritual identity. That vision is a moral quest to reclaim for our children the values, the virtues, and the dreams that are their inheritance as children of God. It is a vision that cannot accept anything less.

In the past few years, my prayers for the children in our society have taken on an urgent tone as the chaos they experience grows. One morning, as I knelt in the chapel at the Catholic Center, I felt a certain sadness that tempted me to despair that things would never change. I looked at Christ on the crucifix, His arms outstretched, and thought, "The children need you to wrap your arms around them and protect them, but sometimes it seems to me as if You have no arms."

About a month after that morning I was at a conference in San Diego. The group I was with planned to meet at one of the old missions for Mass. As I knelt in the dimly lit church, I looked up. There, over the altar, hung a large crucifix. The finely carved figure of Christ that hung on the cross had no arms. I was transfixed. Here, thousands of miles from Memphis hung the armless God of my prayer. What a coincidence. Who would hang a broken cross over the altar and why? After the Mass I asked the priest why the figure had no arms. He told me he found the crucifix buried under a tarp in the corner of a small shop in Rome. In spite of the fact the arms were missing, the wooden figure of Christ was so beautiful and the look on His face so moving, he decided to buy the crucifix, have it restored, and hang it in the Mission. When Father returned to San Diego and the Sisters at the mission saw the crucifix, they convinced him to hang it just like it is, without arms. They said it would remind us all that we are Christ's arms and must do His work in the world.

What a very clear answer to my prayer. You cannot expect someone else to be a parent for you. You cannot clutter your life with more voices telling you how to raise your children. The only voice you need is the one that whispers to your soul, "They are made in the image and likeness of God; to whom else shall you turn?"

> *The only voice you need is the one that whispers to your soul, "They are made in the image and likeness of God; to whom else shall you turn?"*

It is in your faith, and your shared journey with all who touch the lives of the children, that you will renew your hope, reclaim your children, and reinvent your parenting. Turn to God for your answers. Your prayers are an act of faith in the midst of doubt. It is God's grace that will cause you to be heroic parents. He will give you the wisdom to discern the truth. He will give you the courage to transform the world. He will give you the strength to take unprecedented action on behalf of your children. He does have arms. They are yours.

# He Loves You Best

There is a saying, "Small children disturb your sleep, big children your life." That's not a saying you find on birth announcements or balloons tied to doorknobs on the hospital maternity floor. It's a saying for later, after the emotional high that accompanies this new interpersonal relationship called parenthood. It's a saying for after this time when everything seems so glorious. There is a newness that can become seductive and mask the insecurity, the fear of failure, that a person might feel when leaving what is known to go to the unknown, when losing one identity to create a new one. I remember when the reality of being a parent first hit me. It was the day after everyone left. My husband was back at work, our family members and friends had all returned to their homes, and my son and I were alone for the first time since he was born. I looked at this tiny gift of love and thought, "Now what?"

I'm sure it's a common experience. Here we are, people of vast experience, people who have "been there, done that," who know what life is like "out there," away from family and home. How hard can this be after all we have learned? And what do we want to do with that knowledge? We want to pass it on. We'd like to save our children, whom we love, from having to go through the hardships we had to endure because of our mistakes. We'd like to smooth the way, point out the pitfalls, and guide our children over them. We want to keep them safe and out of harm's way. But what happens when we can't? What do we do when they suffer?

I overheard someone ask my mother-in-law years ago, "Which one of your children do you love the best?" Without missing a beat, she replied, "The one that is sick, or farthest from home." Over the years, I have come to understand the wisdom of this truth and the universal essence of compassion. When all is well, when your child throws his arms around you and says, "I love you," when you see your child helping another child, or bursting with excitement at a victory won or a skill learned, when you see your happy and healthy child grow in wisdom and age and grace, then life is beautiful and love unquestionable. But there are those times, no matter how young or old our children are, when you learn that the labels "Child Proof" and "Unbreakable" don't come on a parent's heart.

*It is when our children are sick, or far from home, that we must love them best. Love is stronger than fear or hate or grief.*

So, what happens when things go wrong, when you can't keep them from harm? You give your advice, you counsel, you educate. You tell your children what needs to be done, and they do the opposite. There may be times when they are sick in mind, body, or spirit and you think, "Now what?" There may be times when they are far from home, and you ache for their safe return. There may be times when they are too weak, too tired to fight for recovery or overcome their addictions. There may be times when they have strayed so far from the core of who they are, when their anger, fear, or a violent and hostile world keeps them from returning, and you think "Who is this person, this child of mine?" Where then is the balance between those two halves of your child, the half that can fill your heart with grief and the half that can melt it with love? The balance lies in compassion. It is when our children are sick or far from home, that we must love them best. Love is stronger than fear or hate or grief. It is compassion that suffers with them and relieves their burdens when they are too weak to fight or too blind to find a way home. It is compassion that keeps a light on in the window, waiting in prayer for their safe return. It is compassion that gives them hope for forgiveness and strength for a new beginning.

But it isn't just your child who is entitled to such compassion, to being loved best when he is suffering or lost. This is the birthright of all of us as children of God. At those times in your life when you are sick in mind, body, or spirit, at those times when you are far from home, the home to which we all journey, at those times when you have been beaten down by life, betrayed, or lonely, at those times when hurt gnaws at your heart, it is always a gentle comfort and source of great strength to know, even in the midst of great evil or suffering or loss, that there is a God, a compassionate Father, who waits for your return, who enfolds you in His arms, and who, in His infinite subjectivity, loves you best.

# The Best Years of Your Life

They sat in my office, their eyes glazed over with confusion and concern, talking about their teenage child who was a student at the school where I was Principal. It was a discussion similar to hundreds of others I have had over the years with parents of preteen and teenage children. The symptoms of this adolescent age are ancient and universal. Bubbly conversations are often replaced with monosyllabic grunts and caustic retorts to simple parental questions like "How was your day?" The adoring eyes of childhood now often turn into glaring slits in a pouty face. What happened? And the parents' questions about their teens are just as universal.

"He is so different," they say. "He seems so distant, resentful of our questions, our rules, and the things we always did together as a family."

"There is always a drama going on," others have said, "and we always find ourselves in the middle of it, not even sure why we're so upset."

"She says we're intruding into her life," a mother says.

"He says that these are supposed to be the best years of his life, and we're ruining them," a father moans. "It seems like the worst years of our lives!"

"Keep parenting," I say, "he'll be back," as I hand the parents a copy of a piece I read years ago, when my children were in the throes of that sixth through twelfth grade syndrome. Its author is unknown, but my friends and I passed it around like a recipe for survival, as we traded war stories from those best years of our teenagers' lives.

"Read this. It might help," I say to the parents, as I give them a copy of the following:

# The Cat Years

I just realized that while children are dogs—loyal and affectionate—teenagers are cats. It's so easy to be a dog owner. You feed it, train it, boss it around. It puts its head on your knee and gazes at you as if you were a Rembrandt painting. It bounds indoors with enthusiasm when you call it.

Then around age 13, your adoring little puppy turns into a big old cat. When you tell it to come inside, it looks amazed, as if wondering who died and made you emperor. Instead of dogging your footsteps, it disappears. You won't see it again until it gets hungry—then it pauses on its sprint through the kitchen long enough to turn its nose up at whatever you're serving. When you reach out to ruffle its head, in that old affectionate gesture, it twists away from you, then gives you a blank stare, as if trying to remember where it has seen you before.

You, not realizing that the dog is now a cat, think something must be desperately wrong with it. It seems so antisocial, so distant, sort of depressed. It won't go on family outings. Since you're the one who raised it, taught it to fetch, and stay and sit on command, you assume that you did something wrong. Flooded with guilt and fear, you redouble your efforts to make your pet behave.

Only now you're dealing with a cat, so everything that worked before now produces the opposite of the desired result. Call it, and it runs away. Tell it to sit, and it jumps on the counter. The more you go toward it, wringing your hands, the more it moves away. Instead of continuing to act like a dog owner, you can learn to behave like a cat owner. Put a dish of food near the door, and let it come to you. But remember that a cat needs your help and your affection, too. Sit still, and it will come, seeking that warm, comforting lap it has not entirely forgotten. Be there to open the door for it.

One day your grown-up child will walk into the kitchen, give you a big kiss and say, "You've been on your feet all day. Let me get those dishes for you." Then you'll realize your cat is a dog again.

**It is by no means a coincidence that the only account we have of Jesus as a child is when he was approaching adolescence.**

If there was ever a time that parents need divine inspiration and guidance, it is when they are parents of an adolescent child. Even God's Son exhibited the stereotypical rebellion, posturing, and search for independence that is so much a part of adolescence. And as for His parents, well, some things never change. Just like us, they worried over the behavior of their adolescent child. Their firm, but slightly insecure, admonition was so much like yours. You know what is best, but your teenagers seem so sure of themselves and so determined to do things their way, that you often find yourself questioning your own judgment. Their world seems so foreign to you, sometime even dangerous. And, like Mary and Joseph, you must be firm in your commitment to continue to be parents to your adolescent child, whether he likes it or not.

It is never easy being a parent. But, being a parent of an adolescent is particularly trying. When my children were teenagers, it was always a source of strength for me to recall how Mary and Joseph handled their rebellious teen when he wandered off from a family outing, seeking his independence.

*And, like Mary and Joseph, you must be firm in your commitment to continue to be parents to your adolescent child, whether he likes it or not.*

They "grounded" Him for eighteen years. They must have. The next time we hear of Him, He is thirty years old. That might not work well for you. But at least trust your same God-given intuition and authority as a parent. Claim for yourself what we behold in Mary and Joseph. Parent your child so that he or she will continue to grow in wisdom and age and grace.

When you can look back on these years of parenting teenagers with the wisdom that comes from experience and the confidence that comes from survival, you can then enjoy watching your adult children raise their teenagers. Now those are the best years of your life!

# The Conversation Piece

One evening, while visiting with my daughter, she told me that she had been looking for a "conversation piece" for her home for over a year, but still had not found just the right thing. She asked if I had any ideas. Without hesitation, I asked, "What do you want to talk about?" It was obviously the wrong response. That familiar roll of her eyes indicated that I was clueless when it came to interior decorating. I think she was beginning to be concerned that she might be, too. But then, how could she have hoped to inherit the "Martha Stewart gene" from a mother whose attempts at gardening are limited to occasionally rearranging the fake flowers in the front yard? As she went on to show me pictures of various "conversation pieces," my mind wandered to the things that started some of the most meaningful conversations in our home when she and her brother were growing up.

The crib was certainly a conversation piece. No sooner did my husband and I place our first child in it when the conversations began. They usually centered on our uncertainty as we ventured into parenthood. "He's been crying for hours. What do you think is wrong?" "I don't hear him; check and see if he is breathing." We would lean on the rails of the crib. Sometimes we would just stare at our son, but mostly we would have conversations about what we wanted his life to be like and what we needed to do to give him that life. However grand our dreams for him, we knew that what he needed most was both of us.

There were lots of things that started conversations when the children were young. Like the things on the floor that weren't supposed to be there—food crumbs, a thousand puzzle pieces, spilled milk, wet towels, and too many toys. Those things could always start a conversation. Somehow, those conversations don't seem as significant now as they were then. Clean floors aren't as much fun as the ones strewn with toys. There was, of course, the conversation piece that begged the question, "Whose turn was it to walk the dog?" That piece always started the conversation about responsibility.

As our children entered adolescence, the car keys were always a conversation piece. They were a symbol of freedom for them and a source of concern for us. Their conversations always started with, "Don't you trust me?" And mine ended with, "Love is unconditional; trust, you'll have to earn." It's a difficult lesson to teach and to learn. But children need to learn that trust is a virtue acquired by practicing to be trustworthy. And, while learning, even if they violate the trust now and then, the love is still there. Car keys started many conversations.

*The most important conversation piece in a home is really the family who lives there.*

The crucifixes over the beds were always conversation pieces. They still are. The conversations are with God. They are conversations that start the day and end it. They are the conversations of parents and children. They are about concerns and gratitude, new jobs and new places to live. They are about death and new life, about changes and stages, about hopes and fears. They are conversation pieces that chronicle the life of a family. Now that I think about it, the most important conversation piece in a home is really the family who lives there.

My daughter pointed to a picture in the magazine and asked, "What about this?"

"I don't know," I said. "I kind of like the train set you have on the coffee table. It looks like a family lives here."

She just rolled her eyes. I guess I'll never be a decorator.

# What Did You Learn in School Today?

It was his first day in Second Grade. I was eager to find out how his day went, so I asked my son, Matt, the dreaded question, "What did you learn in school today?"

And he gave me the dreaded response, "Nothing."

"Nothing," I said, wishing I had asked a better question.

"No," he said. "I'm still trying to figure out what I'm supposed to do, so I can do it, and what I'm not supposed to do, so I won't do it. It's not First Grade anymore."

Over the years I have asked that question hundreds of times. Over the years, the answers were sometimes specific, sometimes vague, and sometimes made up, just to keep me from asking again. But my son's answer that first day of Second Grade stays with me. Actually, he learned a lot that day. He learned about acquiring a different perspective. He learned about building the capacity to think and act in a new way. These are very good skills to use in a world of constant revisions. I felt confident in his fitness to survive the changes in his life. He also coined a new saying for me that day, "It's not First Grade anymore!" It is a saying that I sometimes use when I am faced with a new or changing situation. There are times when the student becomes the teacher in that question, "What did you learn in school today?"

Nick Stidham graduated from St. Benedict High School in Memphis, Tennessee, a few years ago. Several years before his graduation he came home from school with an answer to that question, "What did you learn in school today?" It was an answer that became an anchor for Nick, and now, an anchor for his family. Nick had learned that day that "God is good, all the time, and, all the time, God is good." Nick, along with more than 8,000 students and teachers from the Catholic schools in the Diocese of Memphis learned it from Bishop J. Terry Steib, S.V.D., during his homily at the All Schools Mass. The Mass is held as a celebration of the unity and the diversity of the Catholic schools. It is a public witness of our faith and Catholic identity.

During his homily, Bishop Steib taught the children what has since become a mantra for all of us. At one point in his homily, he instructed one side of the arena to call out, "God is Good!" and the other side to respond, "All the time!" The students went back and forth with the chant and loved it. The saying soon appeared on bulletin boards in classrooms, on T-shirts, and even found its way into the conversations of the students and their families. It has become something we say to each other. Nick learned it, he believed it, and he lived it. It became something his family said, every now and then, to emphasize God's goodness, even in the midst of a trying time. They learned it, believed it, and they lived it, too.

Nick died not long after he graduated from St. Benedict. He was killed in a car accident as he tried to avoid a car ahead of him that had gone out of control on a rain-slick road. The accident ended Nick's life, and it began life without Nick for his family. The death of a child is not supposed to happen. The sword that pierces a parent's heart when it does, is the same sword that pierced Mary's heart as she held her Son at the foot of the cross. "How do you go on?" I thought to myself at I sat in the pew at Nick's funeral. I looked down at the prayer card that was given out at the Mass. On the front of the card was a picture of the Sacred Heart of Jesus. I turned it over. On the other side was printed,

*Nicholas Joseph Stidem*
*"God is Good, all the time, and all the time, God is good."*

"Nick would have wanted that on the card," his mother told me after the Mass. "He believed it, and we do, too, even now. God is giving us strength through our faith in Him." What Nick learned in school, at St. Benedict, he shared even in death, so that others will read it and believe.

What did you learn in school, at work, or wherever you were today? What did others learn from you? Maybe all we need to learn, or to teach others, is what Nick learned at the All Schools Mass at school that day. "God is good, all the time, and all the time, God is good."

# Strengthen the Human Chain

When I was growing up, my family would spend the summers at the beach. Learning to swim in the Atlantic Ocean also meant learning to respect the unpredictability of the undertow. I learned that respect after I was pulled from its grasp by the last person on a human chain of rescuers, as I was sucked under the water for what I thought would be the last time. It was an experience I did not want to repeat. I had a choice to make. I could stay on the safety of the shore and ensure that it would never happen again. Or, I could become a stronger swimmer and prepare for the risk. I chose the latter.

How many times in your parenting have you faced choices that have the same effect on you? How many times as parents have you felt "pulled under" by pressures from peers or the media or by the arbitrary dictates of a secular society? You fight to keep your head above the "water" of opinions and do what you feel is right for your children. Yet, sometimes you feel as though you don't have the strength to hold out. It becomes easier and easier to just give up, to go along. It becomes easier to assign blame and offer excuses. It becomes easier to accept what is morally wrong when what is morally wrong becomes the familiar environment and doing what is right becomes the risk. Parents cannot afford to cling to the perceived safety of staying on the shore.

Parents have a choice to make. You can just sit on the sideline and watch society raise your children, or you can become stronger parents and prepare for the risks that you will encounter. Choose the latter. It is not easier. It will require a lot more strength, self-discipline, and patience. But to do otherwise is to deny your ability to parent. You need the strength to unleash your potential to parent. You must have the courage of your convictions and a strong moral code. You need a deep faith in

God. And, you need to pray. God has given you inexhaustible reserves of strength and courage through prayer.

There is something else you need. You need each other. Too often you might be tempted to just give in to the pressures around you and say, "What can I do? I am only one person."

I cannot help but think, "Where would I be had each of the twenty-seven persons on the human chain of rescuers who pulled me out of the ocean felt that way?" Not one of them would have been able to save me alone without getting caught in the undertow. But, by working together, supporting each other, trusting each other, and relying on each other, I was pulled to safety.

*God has given you inexhaustible reserves of strength and courage through prayer.*

Maybe you should take the same approach with your children. Maybe you should seek out others who will join in rescuing the children from all that threatens them, from becoming the person God intends them to be. Perhaps by working together, supporting each other, and relying on one another, your children will be pulled to safety. They are not yet strong enough to save themselves. Teach them how to be stronger persons by exhibiting that strength yourself. It is a strength grounded in prayer, faith, and a willingness to create a human chain of rescuers.

# A History
## with
# GOD

In a life well-lived

# Programmed for Endurance

Not long ago, while waiting in line at the grocery store, I overheard a very weary-looking young father with a baby in his arms and two toddlers sitting in the shopping cart, say to the clerk, "My wife is sick, the kids are sick, the baby was up all night, and work is piling up on my desk. I feel like I'm sixty."

I looked at him and thought, "No, you feel like you are thirty-something with a family to raise and a thousand bells to answer. If you were sixty, you would have gotten a good night's sleep, wondered if your grandchildren's colds were better, and your work would be piling up on someone else's desk." Survival has its rewards. But when you are in the midst of the storm, it is sometimes difficult to even imagine that any calm will follow. It will. Just hold on.

The incident reminded me of a time in my life when I was where that young father is. I had children who were sick and had been up all night. I had work piled up on my desk. I had overextended my obligations to church and civic groups. It was two o'clock in the morning, and I was baking cupcakes for what seemed, at the time, like a very important event. As I stood at the kitchen counter icing the cupcakes, I found myself thinking wistfully about the last real rest I had. It was when I was under anesthesia having surgery.

As strange as it seems, in my exhaustion, came insight. I thought about the times that Christ went off to a quiet place to rest. He programmed His life for endurance. Maybe I should do the same. Perhaps I should trade the excitement of the sprint for the measured pace of the long distance run. If Jesus prioritized the time to rest, leaving the multitudes to be healed, then surely I, too, could cut back on a few of the demands on my time. I needed to immerse myself in some downtime, to rest and pray, to pace myself, even a little, so that I also would be programmed for endurance. If you are always consumed by the things you are doing, then you will lose sight of the person you are becoming. And who you are, not what you do, is what endures.

It takes the grace of God to recognize and treasure the time you have, even when times are tedious and difficult. To remain faithful to the day to day is all you are really called to do. But there may be times when that faithfulness is challenged, when

> *If you are always consumed by the things you are doing, then you will lose sight of the person you are becoming. And who you are, not what you do, is what endures.*

the clamor of the demands on you drowns out the whispers of the soul urging you to things eternal. When you try to please everyone, you please no one, including yourself. When you try to accomplish everything, you accomplish nothing. When you neglect your own needs, you eventually lack the moral and physical stamina you need to become the person God intends you to be. You cannot give what you do not have. What is it that you need in order to meet the challenge of faithfulness to do what you are called to do? Perhaps you need to do what Christ did— rest and pray. If you find this solution impossible to do, then you may need to do it more than you realize. In the meantime, you can ease the overburdened lifestyle with sensitivity to each other's weariness by encouragement, understandin,g and hope and by being wise enough to unburden yourself of your own weariness, so that you have the endurance you need for life's long distance journey.

# A Snake's Tale

If you hear of a contest in the "Well, what did you expect?" category, let me know. I have the winner. I read an article in the newspaper about a man who was almost squeezed to death by his pet snake. Somehow, the boa constrictor worked its way out of its cage in the man's bedroom and wrapped itself around its sleeping owner. The startled man was awakened by the intense pressure as the snake continued to squeeze. His screams alerted his wife who managed to save her husband by killing the snake. The man expressed his sadness and disbelief at the snake's behavior. He was quoted as saying, "He was my friend. What did he do that for?"

Friend or not, it was a snake. What did the guy expect? The article reminded me of a tale I heard years ago, a tale that has, on more than one occasion, allowed me to recognize the contradictions that surround us everyday.

A young girl was walking through the woods on a cold winter day when she heard a voice call out, "Girl, help me!"

She looked down and saw a snake at her feet. The snake cried out, "Please help me. The ground is frozen and I am cold. If I stay down here I will freeze to death. Please pick me up and put me under your coat. It is warm there."

The girl looked at him and said, "No, I cannot pick you up. You are a snake. If I put you under my coat, you will bite me and I will surely die."

"No," said the snake, "I will not bite you, I promise. I just want to stay warm and travel through the woods with you. I am so cold."

The girl looked with pity at the snake. He seemed so harmless as he shivered on the cold ground. Although she knew better, she felt sorry for the snake. In the emotion of the moment, she gave in to his pleas.

"All right," she said, "I'll take you with me and keep you warm. But remember your promise."

So the girl picked up the snake and drew him to her to keep him warm. As she wrapped her coat around him, the snake bit her. She fell to the ground. As her life slipped away, she cried to the snake, "Why did you bite me? You promised you would not hurt me. You lied to me."

"What did you expect?" the snake hissed as he slithered away. "You knew I was a snake when you picked me up."

It happens. Everything you know, all that you believe, is often tested in the only way and in the only time and place available to us. Your test is not in what you believe, but in your response to the contradiction in the present moment, to the temptation before you. What is it that you pick up? What do you draw to you that could corrupt you spiritually, morally, physically, or psychologically? Whom do you trust not to harm you? What situations do you put yourself in that will only serve to destroy you? What do you do that makes you less than who you are? How do you rationalize that your destructive associations really won't hurt you or that bad habits are easy to break? Even the perceived comfort of the status quo can fool you into believing that you are in control. Even your best intentions can deceive you. What snakes have you picked up that seek only to steal your spirit, to destroy your families, your children, your community, your world? What is in our society that lures you with lies? What

> *Your struggles are most clearly seen in the light of faith. It is that faith that gives you the wisdom to judge what you see and experience in the light of what you believe.*

seduces you with smooth talk, with perverse righteousness, that makes wrong seem like right? How do you keep the snakes at bay?

It is difficult to trust in the unseen when you would rather believe what you see and hear in front of you, even if it is a snake. It is our nature to be comfortable in a world we create for ourselves. Yet it is through that transparent humanity that your light shines brightest. Your struggles are most clearly seen in the light of faith. It is that faith that gives you the wisdom to judge what you see and experience in the light of what you believe. It is faith that takes over when your best efforts fail. You cannot eliminate the contradictions in our world. But faith allows you to understand that they exist and that you can live among them without letting them destroy you. What seems like a good thing could be evil. What appears to be counter-culture could be right. It is God's hand that steadies you when you are weakened or made vulnerable by the contradictions in our world. He breaks through your routine to remind you that you are ultimately dependent only upon Him. No matter how many snakes cross your path, He gives you the wisdom to see them for what they are, the strength and courage not to pick them up, and the grace to draw to yourself only Him.

# A Wedding Feast in Memphis

High drama makes for great movies and TV soap operas; however, it is not necessarily something I would choose to shape the events of my own life. During the first few days of February 1996, the unlikely elements of the chaos theory mixed together with the culture of hope to produce, out of apparent disorder, what seemed to be a miracle to rival that of the marriage feast at Cana.

Our daughter's wedding day was heralded by the prediction of six to eight inches of snow to be added to the still frozen accumulation already on the ground. In Memphis, even a hint of a chance of snow is grounds for panic. Guests coming from five countries, sixteen states, and right here in Memphis operated with the fuzzy logic that grows out of yet unrealized possibilities. We all proceeded. I knew that the drastic changes in plans that might be called for would in no way diminish the young couple's lifelong commitment to each other. However, of all the possible outcomes to any wedding, I would have gladly traded snow in Memphis for running out of wine in Cana.

The night before the wedding, many friends and family members were gathered at our house, listening to the latest forecasts. Every TV station carried the same dire prediction: Memphis was in the line of fire for a direct hit by a fierce winter storm that was rapidly approaching. All of those gathered around the TV looked at me as if I had a solution, an idea, a hook to hang hope on. It was way out of my league. I don't do weather.

"There is only one thing to do," I said. "Pray."

So we stopped and prayed for that enclave of goodness in the general chaos, a miracle.

It was through prayer that we could let go of possible outcomes, and embrace the impossible. If Jesus chose a wedding, a very ordinary event, at which to perform His first miracle,

46

then our common, everyday events must be important to Him. Perhaps He would choose another wedding in need of a miracle now. It was at Jesus' mother Mary's suggestion that he changed the water into wine at Cana. I believed that through our prayers for Divine intervention, Mary would suggest that He change six to eight inches of snow into a sunny day. So I prayed, "Tell Him they have no sun."

On February 3, 1996, there was a miracle at another wedding feast. In spite of the fact that record-breaking winter storms engulfed the country, and snow and ice surrounded our city, there seemed to be a wall around Memphis, and the prediction of a 100% chance of snow and ice did not come true. The sun came out. It melted the ice that had accumulated on the ground and melted the hearts of anyone who did not believe in miracles. It was a beautiful day for a wedding. On their way to Memphis at seven that morning, three dear friends stopped on I-40 to take a picture of the sun coming up over the frosty fields outside of Memphis. That picture still hangs on a wall in our den where we all stopped to pray the night before the wedding. It is a dramatic reminder of life, hope, and God's goodness in the dead of winter.

God's miracles are not limited to weddings. You limit your chance to experience His miracles when you deny your culture of faith and hope and prayer, and the importance of that faith and hope and prayer in your everyday life. Pray unceasingly. Pray for the strength to honor the absoluteness of the marriage vow. Pray for the fortitude to parent your children grounded

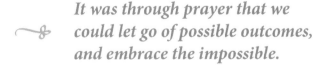

*It was through prayer that we could let go of possible outcomes, and embrace the impossible.*

in wisdom, truth, and love. Pray for the courage to exemplify for others the constancy of the values of family life, and to encourage others by your example of faith and hope. Pray for the healing of mind, body, and spirit so desperately needed for yourself or others. Pray for that divisive situation at your work, or in your family, that is causing pain for so many. Pray to find employment, to find acceptance, to find peace. Even if you think there is no way, pray and trust God to make a way.

It is the words of Jesus Himself that strengthen your faith:

> When he entered the house, the blind men approached him and Jesus said to them, "Do you believe that I can do this?"
>
> "Yes, Lord," they said to him.
>
> Then he touched their eyes and said, "Let it be done for you according to your faith." (Matthew 9:28-30)

Pray also for the wisdom to give God the final decision on all your prayers and your plans. I cannot begin to understand the depth of the mystery of God's presence in our lives. I only know that He loves us, delights in doing things for us, and asks nothing more than trust from us. We all have stories of God's surprises, His miracles, in our lives. Freely share your miracles. There are plenty more where they came from, and sometimes they even happen at wedding feasts.

# Are You Listening?

We have become a society that has raised multitasking to an art form. At a recent meeting I attended, one of the members of the group was bragging that he had just finished talking on the phone while responding to e-mails at the same time. The man next to him asked, "Was it a conference call?"

Then he went on to boast, "I can do a conference call, answer my e-mail, and be meeting with someone in my office, all at the same time."

What dubious distinctions. I wonder if anyone was listening? What if all the others involved were doing the same thing?

It is said that imitation is the sincerest form of flattery. Actually, I think listening is. To be truly present to another person is more than flattering. It is love in action. It is a respect that comes from reverence and a sense of awe when encountering the unique mystery of another person. Listening restores ceremony to the empty ritual of just talking. A speaker needs a listener. Connectedness to others happens through our feelings and emotions when we listen, unconditionally. It has nothing to do with judging, or agreeing, or even liking. It is about acceptance, about understanding, and about the spirituality of presence. It is about just being there for another person.

Words are made flesh when they bring meaning, when they create community and make our experiences truly human. Listening to the words of others, and others listening to our words, can bring healing, reconciliation, understanding, peace, joy, insight, consolation, comfort, and hope. To listen is to love. It is the kind of love we read about in 1 Corinthians, Chapter 13. In fact, if we substituted the word "listening" for the word "love," it would go something like this:

> *Listening* is the gift of love. Now I will show you a way which surpasses all others. *Listening* is patient:

49

with children who ask endless questions, with friends who just need to talk, with a grandparent who tells the same story over and over again. *Listening* is kind: it appreciates the trust of a secret, it responds in compassion to the pain of another, it accepts the need of another to share his or her story. *Listening* is not jealous of the accomplishments or happiness of others, but responds in joy. *Listening* is not snobbish. It does not put on airs. It does not criticize the grammar while missing the message. It seeks to communicate and to create community in the lived human experience. *Listening* is never rude. It does not judge what is in the heart or mind or thoughts of another. It seeks to understand. One who is listening hears only the words spoken by another, not the words in his mind that are waiting to be spoken. *Listening* is not prone to anger, but recognizes the trust of another as he seeks to share his thoughts and feelings, and bring meaning to his actions. *Listening* does not rejoice in what is wrong, but rejoices in the truth, and, when hearing it, affirms all who speak it. *Listening*, truly listening to another, has the calming rhythm of a rocking chair, not the frantic pace of a multitasking society.

It is interesting to think that if we take the risk of just listening to another person and responding in love to what we hear, we might realize that what we do in the simple act of listening will live on in the hearts, minds, and lives of all those who remembered that we listened.

# Feathers in the Wind

A dmiral Rickover was quoted as saying, "Great minds discuss ideas. Average minds discuss events. Small minds discuss people."

Years ago, I heard about a woman who was noted for her "small mind." She was intelligent and held a position of authority, but her mantra seemed to be, "If you can't say anything nice about someone, then sit next to me." Her judgmental approach was so subtle that she didn't really have to say too much at all. All she had to do was plant a seed of doubt about the ability or character or lifestyle of her latest target in the mind of her listener. She knew, or so the story goes, that this was a shortcoming, and so one day during Lent, she decided to wipe the slate clean and mend her ways.

She went to her parish priest to seek forgiveness, confess her sins, and start over. When she was finished with her confession, the priest handed her a large feather pillow and told her to take it, cut it open, go to the middle of the Old Bridge and shake the feathers out of the pillow. When there were no more feathers left in the pillow, she was to bring the empty pillowcase back to him. It sounded like a strange penance to her, but she did as she was instructed. When she returned to the priest, she handed him the pillowcase. With the exception of some feathers clinging to the woman's clothes and hair, all the feathers were gone.

"Now," said the priest, "go back and gather up all the feathers and put them back in the pillowcase."

The woman was shocked at the impossibility of the task. "There is no way I can do that; they have blown away. I don't know where they went. They went everywhere. I will never be able to get them back."

"You are right," the priest said, "and neither will you be able to get back even a single word of gossip about another person, or collect all the seeds of doubt that you have planted in the minds

51

of others that have already started to germinate. The only thing that will remain," the priest continued, "is the reputation that clings to you, like the feathers on your clothes and hair. Now, brush them off and start over, but remember the experience of the feather pillow."

And the woman left, changed by the experience, transformed by the crisis of understanding.

"A perverse person stirs up conflict, and a gossip separates close friends" (Proverbs 16:28).

"Without wood a fire goes out; without a gossip a quarrel dies down" (Proverbs 26:20).

The Gossip manipulates the thoughts of others to serve a self-promoting need. The focus narrows only on that need and does not see the "big picture," the interconnectedness of us all. When you wound, you are wounded. When you heal, you are healed. When you lift up another person, you are lifted. When you are committed to a spiritual evolution, you come to understand that you are tethered, one to another, by God's love, and your words frame your commitment to live in that love.

> *When you are committed to a spiritual evolution, you come to understand that you are tethered, one to another, by God's love, and your words frame your commitment to live in that love.*

If you are ever tempted to throw words, like the feathers in the wind, you should make sure that your words would be considered as coming from a "great mind" and pleased that some would cling to you.

# How Hard Can It Be?

It was a very large high school located in the inner city of Philadelphia. The challenges at the school mirrored the challenges in the neighborhood, and the struggles of those who were just trying to make it through another day. It was my first day of teaching. "How hard can it be?" I thought as I waited in my classroom for the first bell to ring. I had been in school most of my life. I had seen dozens of teachers. They were in charge, explained material, and gave homework. "I can do that," I thought, "how hard can it be?"

Then the students came in. I quickly learned how hard a job can be. By the end of the day, I had taught six classes of Algebra and Geometry to about 230 students, none of whom wanted to be in that class. Added to that was the warning from my colleagues that the first day is always as good as it gets. "I'm in big trouble," I thought. "Now what?" I was not eager to face the next day, not to mention the coming year. Yet I knew that I was supposed to be there. I believed it was where God had called me to be, so, like it or not, I was just going to face it. I soon learned that the students needed more than Math. The problems they faced were more than just finishing their homework. They needed to experience hope and a vision for their future that was more than their experience of the present told them it would be. I began to understand why I was there. My job was to teach the students Math. My mission was to be a conduit of God's love for them, to change the environment for them, even for an hour a day, so that they would learn to grow in that love. I was prepared for the job, but needed anointing for the mission.

Jesus knows what you are made of. He tells you what it will take for you to succeed in His mission, in spite of frustration, fear, or failure. It is prayer. It is through prayer that God anoints you for times of trouble. In the Gospel of Matthew, Jesus makes it clear that even if your job is difficult to do, when you are fulfilling God's plan for your life, prayer will strengthen you for your mission, and keep you doing your job.

> He advanced a little and fell prostrate in prayer, saying, "My Father, if it is possible, let this cup pass from me; yet, not as I will, but as you will."
>
> When he returned to his disciples he found them asleep. He said to Peter, "So you could not keep watch with me for one hour? Watch and pray that you may not undergo the test. The spirit is willing, but the flesh is weak." (Matthew 26:39-41)

It is the same for you when it is hard to do whatever it is you do. Often God will use adversity in your life to bring about good, to use a difficult situation to fulfill His purpose. If there is a problem, then perhaps you have been chosen by God to be the solution. Perhaps you are meant to be the blessing in a hostile environment, and to make a difference by not becoming part of it. There is a reason you are in that job, that family, that situation. When you are anointed, empowered by the Holy Spirit for your mission, then you can work with the difficult people no one else can work with. You can raise the children no one else can raise. You can teach the students no one else can teach. You can work with the customers no one else can work

*Jesus knows what you are made of. He tells you what it will take for you to succeed in His mission, in spite of frustration, fear, or failure. It is prayer.*

with. You can handle the situations no one else can handle. You can change the environment that destroys other people. You can work with the finances no one else can manage. You can bear the suffering, the sorrow, or the pain no one else can bear.

Through prayer your faith activates, and you are at your best when the situation is at its worst. You know that God is always your present help in trouble.

How hard can it be? It can be very hard, seemingly impossible at times. If you prepare each day in prayer, you know that with God, all things are possible. God knows your trouble. He knows how you live. He knows where you work. He knows your situation. He knows how hard it can be. Consider Father Mychal Judge's job. He learned how hard it can be to be a Chaplain for a fire department. He did his job, and always remembered his mission. He was prepared for his job, and anointed for his mission. Each day before he went to work, he always said this prayer.

> Lord, take me where you want me to go;
> Let me meet who you want me to meet;
> Tell me what you want me to say,
> And
> Keep me out of your way.

Father Judge was killed on September 11, 2001, at the World Trade Center in New York, while doing his job for the New York City Fire Department and fulfilling his mission for God. May God find you so faithful to the mission He gives you, especially when you find out just how hard it can be.

# I Should Have Stayed In Egypt

What shall we eat? What shall we drink? Did you bring us all the way out into the desert just to die? Is the Lord with us or not? As he led the Israelites out of Egypt to the land God had promised to them, Moses was besieged with doubts, theirs and his. Even though he calmed their fears, interceded with the Lord on their behalf, and solved their latest problem, they continued to whine, complain, and get out of control. "So Moses cried out to the LORD, 'What shall I do with this people? A little more and they will stone me!'" (Exodus 17:4).

It was a pretty scary situation wandering around the desert, lost, with an angry mob nipping at his heels. I can picture Moses now, sitting on a rock in the middle of nowhere saying, "I should have stayed in Egypt. At least in Egypt I had a steady job, some friends to call, and plenty to eat and drink. Whose idea was this anyway? I was riding high in Egypt. Now, I'm up to my ears in chaos. Your promises are great Lord. It's just that the process getting to the promise is challenging. How do I make it through? I should have just stayed in Egypt."

Did you ever get to a dark place in your life, a desperate situation, a hostile environment, and see no way out? Have you ever gone from a sense of wholeness and peace, to feelings of fragmentation and despair? It is easy to have faith when all is well, but life can throw a punch that you would not believe. It can knock you down. When it does, when you find yourself, like Moses, at a breaking point, it is God who picks you up, who stabilizes you in the midst of the struggles, the challenges, the adversity, the illness, the loneliness, the betrayal, or the hostile environment. It is God who transforms what seems like a disaster into a promised new beginning. Sometimes it is difficult to remember that when there is a problem, there is also a promise. It is a promise from God to make a way where there is no way, to keep you on His path no matter how many wrong turns you take. We, like Moses, must love God enough to endure the process in order to get to the promise. It is a promise that God has in store on the other side of chaos, a promise that will lift us up.

Moses wasn't the first. He won't be the last. There are times when all of us, each in our own way, sit in the midst of a storm and wonder, "Where is God in all this? Where is God in this situation, this relationship, this job, this marriage, this ministry, this illness, these bills, this temptation, this betrayal, this hostile environment?" There are times when it seems as if you go from one crisis to another, barely able to catch your breath in between. You can't go back to a comfort zone of the past. You don't see any hope for the future. You wonder how you got into this situation and how do you get out. How do you continue to function, to go on, to continue the journey across your own desert?

*God keeps His promise in the chaos of the process, however impossible your situations seems, so that He can bless you with a new creation within you.*

When you feel as if you can go no farther, when you doubt your purpose and God's plan, when you long to return to a safer time and place, when you just want to cry out, "I should have stayed in Egypt!" remember Moses. Even though his journey in the desert took a lot longer than he anticipated, God provided and was with him every step of the way. God provides you, too, with the resources you will need, with the people you will need, with the solutions you will need. God keeps His promise in the chaos of the process, however impossible your situations seems, so that He can bless you with a new creation within you. And you, like Moses, will know the promise of the Lord: "I myself... will go along, to give you rest" (Exodus 33:14).

# Practice Makes Perfect

When I was in Third Grade, there was a saying posted in the front of the classroom that read, "Practice Makes Perfect." I read it so many times that eventually it became a way of approaching every task, a way of thinking for me. So I practiced achieving that goal of perfection. I practiced spelling words, math problems, and my lines in plays. I practiced playing chess, basketball, and the violin. Once, I even practiced carrying a cake. That was the time I learned about being perfect.

Each year the school celebrated the Pastor's birthday by holding an assembly to "surprise" him with a cake and sing "Happy Birthday." When I was in Fifth Grade, I was chosen to carry the cake to present to Father. For days before the event, I practiced carrying a cake down the thirteen steps from the first floor of the school to the basement hall. I wanted to be perfect, and practice would ensure that.

The day finally arrived. I stood on the landing at the top of the stairs. The Pastor was seated in a chair below. The thousand plus students started to sing. I was three steps into my decent when I tripped. I managed to regain my balance and a firm hold on the plate, but the cake took flight. The singing turned into a collective gasp and, in what can only be described as very slow motion, the cake rotated in mid-air and landed right in the Pastor's lap. The silence was deafening as the Pastor, covered in cake, rose from his seat and ascended the stairs. When he reached the step where I stood, frozen, he put his arm around my shoulders, turned to the crowd, and with a booming voice said, "Now that's what I call a birthday surprise!" Everyone cheered. That's when I learned about perfection. In that compassionate gesture, I learned that being perfect does not feel as good as being loved. I learned that perfection is not the goal—love is.

Love happens in the ordinary events of daily life. It catches us by surprise when it comes disguised as kindness, as compassion, as a whisper of encouragement. Society seems to dictate that only what is perfect is worth having, worth loving. You are told that perfection brings love, and the more perfect you are, the more you achieve, the more you have, the more you are loved. Nothing could be farther from the truth when that kind of perfection becomes the goal.

*In that compassionate gesture,*
*I learned that being perfect does not*
*feel as good as being loved. I learned*
*that perfection is not the goal—love is.*

I don't really believe that practice makes you perfect, but it makes you a lot better than you were before you practiced. Continual improvement is a worthy goal, even when keeping your eyes on the prize is difficult in a world filled with distractions and challenges. If you feel as if you still have a long way to go, getting there is easier when you discover what it is you really should practice. Practice prayer. Practice letting go of specific outcomes. Practice trusting God to light the path traveled. Even if you don't see the perfect way, He does. I have learned that sometimes what we really want is not perfection, but a hug, and someone to appreciate our efforts. It is encouraging if, on occasion, that happens. But it is uplifting to know that with God, it happens all the time. Practicing that does not make you perfect, but rather, perfected in Him whose love is perfect.

# Say You're Sorry

While waiting in the check-out line at the grocery store the other day, I was being entertained by the antics of the two children in front of me. The scene, and the theme, were all too familiar to me. It was a long line, and the children's patience had obviously disappeared before they and their mother got in it. Just for amusement, the little boy whacked the little girl over the head with a loaf of bread.

I have not, that I can remember, ever been hit with a loaf of bread, but I doubt that the wailing that followed was caused by the blow. The mother glared at the little boy and said, "Say you're sorry to your sister."

The boy hissed "Sorry" through his clenched teeth. The girl had that "got you" look on her face as her tears suddenly dried up. About three seconds later, the little girl picked up the loaf of bread and whacked her brother over the head. Now, it was his turn to wail. "Say you're sorry," the mother said.

"He hit me first!" was the response of the little girl. There was obviously no real remorse going on and definitely no forgiveness.

I remember those days. I also remember the "Say you're sorry" command. I think if I had to do it over again, I would not focus on the apology, but on the forgiveness. It is a much more realistic preparation for life, and for heaven. A wise and dear friend told me that forgiveness comes from a forgiving spirit within us, not from an apology from someone else. I believe that. Hearing someone say "Sorry" does not guarantee forgiveness. Forgiveness cannot be lived from the outside in, but from the inside out. I even met someone who proved it by the story of his life.

Several years ago, while waiting for an elevator at an office building, I struck up a conversation with a friendly man who was delivering a pair of freshly shined shoes to one of the offices. It was a short elevator ride and a very brief conversation, but it was one of those tiny rays of sun in an otherwise cloudy day. As I got off the elevator, he called after me, "Stop by my Shoe Shine stand if you're ever on the Lower Level." It was one of those days when I felt like I was on the lower level, covered over by too much to do. The man's cheerfulness seemed so contagious that on my way out, I felt an urge to stop by his stand. As I approached, he was sitting in the chair, waiting for customers. I reminded him of his invitation to stop by. He seemed delighted for the chance to talk. I learned that his name was Eddie. He grew up poor, in Memphis, but worked hard in school and after high school graduation, worked just as hard at his sales job. He was on the way up in life. He got a big promotion and moved to Chicago. He had a great job, earned great money, and had a great life.

All that changed one night as he left a restaurant in downtown Chicago. He was robbed, savagely beaten, and left for dead. After a long hospitalization, and a slow recovery, Eddie returned to Memphis so that his elderly father could take care of him. But he was never the same. Physically, he struggled to walk, experienced a great deal of pain, and always wore a baseball cap to cover the large indentation in his skull. Spiritually, he found God in his suffering and in his life. Once again, he is on the way up. He has his own business now and still works hard. He continually thanks God for the gift of life. I asked him what happened to the men who did this to him. "I never saw them again," he said, "but I forgave them long ago." He forgave them. There was no apology, no remorseful or mandated "sorry" from them. He just forgave them. He forgave them so that he could move beyond what they had done. He did not relive their offenses to him in his heart or in his life.

When I left, he gave me a favorite book of prayers. I gave him an angel pin to wear on his cap. Whenever I stop by his stand, he is always ready with a smile and a sermonette. Both always lift my spirits and make me appreciate the freeing gift of a forgiving spirit. What frees us of hurt is not the "say you're sorry" from someone else, but the "I forgive you" that we live out in our hearts and lives, with or without an apology.

# Show Me Your Friends

There is a saying I grew up hearing that seemed to be a mantra of the authority figures in my life: "Show me your friends and I'll tell you what you are." I would use it myself to caution or encourage my own children as they learned the difference between negative alliances and true friendships. The older I get, the more I think about that saying, and the more I reflect on those in my life I call friends whether lifelong, recent, or somewhere in between. I have come to the realization that I love my friends, not just for who they are, but for who I am because of them.

Even in a world where relationships are scattered and mobile, there is a richness added to your lives by the friendships you have cultivated along the way. It is a richness that cannot be lessened, even when you are separated from friends by distance, or years, or the demands of a life that leaves you with too little time. It is a seamless garment of caring that binds you together, wherever you are. Whether they "knew you when" or met you last year, friends are for all of the seasons of your lives. Friendships are relationships built on mutual trust and on an intensity of love and appreciation, transparency and openness, that is shared with those who are close to your heart.

Friends share goals, growing pains, and insecurities. And no matter what anyone else says, the only label a friend ever gives you is "friend." They tell you the truth, they define who you are, and they hold you accountable for being your best. Because of them you learn, you risk, you grow. Friends help you to make decisions that shape you into being what you were made for, what you were born to be. Their love lifts you, supports you, understands you, is patient with you, forgives you, and asks for forgiveness from you. Friends give you a different perspective, and challenge you to commit to continuous improvement in mind, body, and spirit. Their laughter delights, their passion inspires, and their prayers bring peace. They remind you of your sense of purpose when all seems lost. They live with you in your present circumstances, be they tragic or triumphant, always compassionate, always your biggest fan, and always with an eye towards your future.

Like the Good Samaritan, friends notice your needs and always leave you better off than when they found you. Friends do for you what you cannot do for yourself, like the man in the Bible whose friends helped him by lifting up his stretcher and lowering it through the roof of the house where Jesus was staying, so that Jesus could see the man and be healed. Without a little help from his friends, the man would have missed getting to know Jesus. And, like Jesus, our model of friendship, friends sometimes lay down their lives for you. Not necessarily physically, but often in your time of need, friends drop everything to be with you. And, like Jesus, you still love your friends, even when they, on occasion, betray you, don't understand what you are about, or fall asleep on you just when you are getting to the point of your story. Like Jesus, you see your friends with the eyes of your heart and remember them to God in prayer.

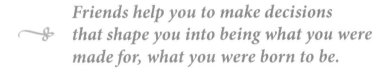

*Friends help you to make decisions that shape you into being what you were made for, what you were born to be.*

Now, when I hear someone say, "Show me your friends and I'll tell you what you are," I think, "I don't need you to tell me what I am. I know what I am because of my friends. I am blessed!" May you always cherish the blessing of friends in your life. May you remember to thank God, and them, for their friendship.

# Appreciate a Faithful Compass

St. John Vianney, the patron saint of parish priests, was a deeply spiritual man, much loved for his compassion, his faithfulness, and for his inspirational preaching. In spite of his popularity, however, he was not appreciated by everyone. There were those who were jealous of his success and mocked his ministry. Shortly after his arrival at a parish as the new pastor, St. John was asked by several women in the parish if he would say Mass one day a week for their special intention. The priest agreed, and faithfully he said Mass each week for their intention, and faithfully they attended the Mass. After fourteen years, when the intention had still not been granted, St. John asked the women if they would share their special intention with him. One woman spoke up and said, "We have been praying that you'd be sent to a different parish."

In spite of outward appearances, it should come as no surprise that we are not always on the same page in our thinking. In spite of our best efforts to communicate, many times we are not even reading the same book. In this diversity of viewpoints in understanding, there are times when the best we can hope to do is to live in the wisdom of uncertainty, trying to put the principles in which we believe at the center of our actions, regardless of how we are judged by others. In our sensitivity to multiple relationships, we discover that we are all wounded in some way and that we are all seeking to be healed.

Our world is created within relationships. It is through our relationships that we learn who we are, what we can do, and what we can become. To be appreciated in a relationship forges identity, heals wounds, and makes us whole again. Appreciation determines in our minds what is real and valuable and what makes us worthy. It is in being appreciated that goals become important. Appreciation acknowledges not only how we succeed, it also recognizes how we contribute, how we remain faithful, and how we influence others. In seeking to set a strong moral compass in our children, it is the appreciation of their attempts at moral courage that matters most. To encourage another to stick to his or her beliefs in the face of overwhelming criticism, great adversity, or fainthearted friends is to set a course that leads to right judgment. It encourages an identity that is rooted in faithfulness to the truth, even against all odds, or when lies come dressed as the truth. It is not enough to tell young people to "just say no" to that which is wrong. It is more important for

*It is through our relationships that we learn who we are, what we can do, and what we can become.*

us to appreciate their attempts at faithfulness to do that which is right. No one gets it right all the time. The best we can do is faithfully keep trying, no matter how long it takes, no matter how we are treated by others, no matter how many times we fail. As Mother Teresa said, "God called us not to be successful, but to be faithful." The world has become a frightening place, even for the most lionhearted among us. For the children, it is even more dangerous. It is not enough to protect them from it. We must make them strong enough to live in it, and courageous enough to seek to make it a better place. They will learn to do what they are appreciated for doing. Who will they learn from if not us?

I am not sure what happened to St. John Vianney and the women parishioners with the special intention. I imagine he continued to faithfully say Mass for their intention, and they faithfully continued to pray for his transfer. Somehow though, because I like happy endings, I believe that the women were touched by his moral courage in the face of adversity, and his faithfulness to do what he was called to do. And that God gave St. John Vianney, as He gives to all of us, the strength to faithfully keep going, even when we know that there are those who are faithfully praying for our demise.

# Teaching Pigs to Sing

My father had an incredible knack for summing up volumes of an entire philosophy in just one sentence. While I was growing up, I did not always appreciate the wisdom hidden in his advice. In fact, I usually found it annoying and would have preferred that he just give me a straight answer, one I didn't have to think about to ferret out a meaning. But I never could change him or his way of responding. Perhaps that is why I have come to understand, and value, his favorite advice to me: "Never try to teach a pig to sing; it will only frustrate you and annoy the pig."

There were more than a few times in my life that I had to relearn that lesson. It is part of the human condition to be tempted to think that if we just try a little harder, we can change another person. It is not good enough that a person is made in the image and likeness of God, so we set about making someone over in the image and likeness of someone more easily understood, more easily controlled, more like us.

In your relationships, you sometimes find yourselves trying to change someone else so that he or she will behave more like you, or conform to your expectations. You might find yourself wanting to "fix" another person in order to change a situation. If a relationship with a spouse, a child, a friend, or a coworker is not working or is causing conflict, you might go to great lengths to find ways to erase the conflict without even identifying its source. Avoiding the issue, or the person, or denying that the conflict really exists, could be the strategy of choice for you. Often, you blame other influences for causing the conflict. More often than not, you convince yourself that if you could just "fix" the other person, the conflict would be resolved. In the attempt of a quick fix of another, you find yourself making elaborate rules, structures, and reward systems. You reason, you imply, you command, you exemplify, you preach, you trick, you whine.

You do everything but recognize the truth. The truth is that no matter what you do you cannot "fix" another person. If he doesn't want to change, you can't change him. If he doesn't want a relationship, you can't make it happen. If he insists on being himself, you can't make him into someone else. No matter how hard you try, you can't make a pig sing, nor can you make your own song pleasurable to the pig.

Sometimes you know that what another person is doing could be harmful physically, morally, spiritually, or professionally to the self or to others. At these times, it is a spiritual work of mercy to admonish, counsel, or suggest. But none of that guarantees a change in another person. You need to realize that we are not responsible for another's behavior. You are responsible only for how you respond to it. And, in your response, you have a great opportunity to demonstrate true Christian behavior. The heart of your response should be recognizing God's perspective on your relationships or situations in which there is conflict and asking, "What can I learn about myself in this?" Instead of focusing on another person, if you focus on yourself and your response, and look beyond the present situation, you will be able to establish a meaningful connection to another that will heal instead of wound. If there is to be a change, the only one you should be concerned about changing is yourself. And that change should liberate the spirit of another.

Often, your only response is prayer. Pray for a change of heart or of perspective. Pray for the wisdom to step back and allow another to grow by using his or her own resourcefulness and purpose. When you allow God to work all things together for good, you begin to understand that the squeals of a pig may not sound like singing to you, but it does to the pig, and to God.

My father was right. Maybe what will remove frustration from our relationships, what we need to fix most, is our appreciation of the song of another, and the way it is sung.

# The Conversation

The drive to the meeting was inspirational. You know, it was one of those times when the weather was perfect, all the lights were green, someone let me in the line of traffic right before it merged to the left. Even the song on the radio inspired me to newness of thought as I weighed possible solutions to the problem being considered at the meeting. I wondered what insights the others attending would offer to the situation. By the time I arrived at the meeting, my thoughts were of nothing else but the potential solutions that always lie hidden in the core of any problem. Before the meeting started, I took my place at the table and looked down at the agenda. There was no discussion planned. It was just a report of what had been, what is, and what will continue to be. I saw that the boundaries had already been established "in the interest of time." The possibilities for excellence that come from shared risk-taking had been relinquished in favor of the safety of mediocrity. The potential that lies in the heart of every conversation was lost to preconceived limitations. The agenda did not unite our effort, but rather separated our thoughts in order to maintain the status quo. The agenda reminded me of the old saying, "If you always do what you always did, then you'll always get what you always got." I picked up my pen and added an item to the agenda, "What do you think?"

Collective wisdom seems to be less and less important in society today. Yes, we have more ways to communicate than ever before, but communication has become one of the simultaneous things that you do as you multi-task, and instant messages have replaced our conversations. How do you get to really know each other, share your thoughts, and be truly connected if your conversations are only brief, superficial, and one-dimensional? How do you build a community, a family, a life, with such short-term focus on relationships? If, in your own lives, on your agendas, on to-do lists, you do not provide time for an encounter with the thoughts, feelings, and ideas of others, then you miss the opportunity to experience the unique perspective each person brings to the whole of life. You will miss the conversation that flows into the rest of your life and inspires you to find purpose and meaning. Short cut communication, at home, at work or in the community, only causes you to know less and assume more. You'll never get to say, "Let's talk about it…what do you think about…you just gave me a great idea…I understand."

You'll never convince me that Starbucks is successful because of the coffee. I believe that they set themselves apart from the competition, not because of the coffee they sell, but because they sell a lifestyle; they portray an image of good conversations happening around the tables. It's a lifestyle of being with others. It is a lifestyle we all want. We want to be together. We want to sit down and talk to each other. We want interconnectedness and relationships. All great ideas started with a conversation. You don't need coffee drinking as an excuse to do this. You don't need agendas to plan your thoughts. You don't need conference tables or dining room tables. You just need to take the time to have the conversation. You want your ideas heard. You want to hear the thoughts of others. Child or adult, you want to have a real conversation, a face-to-face, all-the-time-in-the-world kind of conversation, because you're worth it.

Jesus knew the power a conversation can have when He encountered two men walking on the road to Emmaus. "He asked them, 'What are you discussing as you walk along?'" (Luke 24:17). Then the three began a conversation. By the time they parted company with Jesus, the two friends asked each other, "Were not our hearts burning (within us) while he spoke to us and opened the scriptures to us?"(Luke 24:32). When was the last time you had a conversation that left you "fired-up," inspired you with a call to action, to a vision of what could be? When was the last time you had a conversation that left you with a feeling of connectedness? When was the last time you took the time to start one?

# The Junk Drawer

It's one of those things that just about everyone has, but not everyone is willing to admit to it. I know. I have one. Try as I might to eliminate it from my life, I have finally decided to make peace with the fact that I am a "junk drawer" person. It started out as a drawer. It was just a place to put some of the really important stuff until I could get to it. In it, I could always find pictures of people waiting for identification, important phone numbers without names, directions to an unidentified place, and a jar of baby teeth (my children's, I assume). As our family grew, so did the contents of the "junk drawer."

At different times, I cleaned out the drawer. The contents were accorded the status of "Junque" and relocated to a box. The box eventually became boxes. The boxes became the attic. Now, after forty-four years of marriage, the attic has the potential of becoming an addition on the house in which to store all that really important stuff until I can get to it. There is really nothing wrong with having a "junk drawer." There is, however, something wrong with putting your life in it.

"Junk drawers" are one thing. If need be, they are very disposable. "Junk lives" are another, very different thing. It seems that today, people's lives are stretched thin, and often torn apart, by being pulled in so many different directions. Living in the moment is more complicated when the demand of the next moment is already upon you. You simply have too much to do. You might find yourself constantly setting, and re-setting, your priorities. You make decisions about what to do now and what to put off until you can get to it, regardless of how important it is. Often, what goes in the personal junk drawer of your lives is lost, or forgotten, in a much too busy life. What if that "drawer" becomes filled with the really important stuff you should be doing for yourself?

What have you put in your junk drawer lately? What are the priorities you have set by what you do now, and what you put off doing? Everything in your life—your faith, your family, your work, your friends, your health, your solitude—is clamoring for your attention. How do you "downsize" when nothing seems indispensable? How do you prioritize when everything seems to be a priority? Or is it? There will always be a great deal to do. There will always be hundreds of hours worth of "should." Since there are still only 24 hours in a day, something is definitely being put in your junk drawer. Chances are what you need most is what you are hiding away, saving it to do later, when you can get to it.

If you always cater to the enormous needs of the many others in your life, it may not be possible to have the inner peace and strength you need to fulfill the promise of your own journey. You cannot give what you don't have. Before you empty yourself for others, you need to make sure you have filled yourself with the resources to do so. Even Jesus needed time alone for the R&R He found in prayer and solitude. He even calmed a storm so that He could just rest His eyes for a little while. If you feel as if you are about to crash from the turbulence in your life, maybe it's time you put the oxygen mask on yourself first, take a deep breath, and use your renewed energy to attend to the priority of yourself.

Breathe in the oxygen of prayer, of faith, and of a peace that will give you a right-beneath-the-surface tranquility. It will give you a greater sense of God's presence. There will still be a lot to do, but it will be okay when you have placed your life in God's hands to be lifted up, and not in the junk drawer to be lost in the clutter of a much too busy lifestyle. It is not selfish to recognize the need for personal rejuvenation and the time needed to become a strong person, physically, emotionally, and spiritually. Maybe all the "stuff" in our junk drawers really is important. How will you ever know if you never take the time to find out what the "stuff" really is? Clean it out. Start over. Box up the clutter and give it to God. Begin each day in prayer and let God help you set your priorities so that you will know what is really important, and what can go in the junk drawer.

# The Original Excuse

I know when it all started. It was in the Garden of Eden. It has come to my attention, however, that it was much more than just the effects of the Original Sin that we inherited from Adam and Eve. We also inherited the effects of the Original Excuse: "It's not my fault." The Original Sin got us into this human condition, but it is the Original Excuse that keeps us there.

God very clearly pointed out a specific tree and instructed Adam and Eve not to eat the fruit from that tree. There was no mistaking this tree for another. God probably posted "no trespassing" signs all over the place just as a reminder. Unfortunately for us, God finds Adam eating the forbidden fruit. He caught him right in the act, no way out. It was at that moment that Adam initiated our innate desire to cling to the illusion of control over the situations in which we sometimes find ourselves by assigning responsibility for our wrong actions to someone else. First, Adam blamed God, "The woman whom you put here with me." In other words, if God had not created this other being none of this would have happened. Then he blamed Eve, "she gave me fruit from the tree." In other words, if she had not given it to Adam it would have never even crossed his mind to look at that tree. Eve, sensing this new art of ego-preservation, pointed her finger to the next scapegoat, "The serpent tricked me into it, so I ate it." In other words, the Devil made me do it. (Genesis 3:12-13)

It must have been that Original Excuse that incurred God's wrath. It did not come from their offense towards God, but rather the self-destruction that resulted from their disobedience. He already knew they had disobeyed Him before He asked. Parents are like that. They really don't want answers to those "Now what have you done?" questions as much as they want to hear their children accept responsibility for their actions and perhaps even apologize. So God did what a parent who keeps

His promises does; He followed through with the consequences of their choice, gave them the time and space they needed to learn to accept responsibility for their actions, and then left the light on for their return home, all for the good of His children.

Now, here we are, eons later, still coming up with our own excuses, some quite clever, for not accepting responsibility for our actions. What we learn is that we will never be free to try again, to start over, to forgive or be forgiven until we can let go of the Original Excuse, "It's not my fault." The reality is that our society has only succeeded in getting better at pointing fingers. We have raised this culture of blame to an art form. What a list! We blame everything from what side of the bed we got out on, to what kind of day our hair is having. It's not your fault; it's the fault of your peers, your parents, your job, your spouse, the weather, the way you were raised, the person who cut in front of you. It's not your fault; he started it, it's a habit, they lied to me, and, of course, the devil made me do it. Excuses, however comfortable, justified, or vindicated they make us feel, don't change anything. They only keep us from starting over, from becoming the people we were meant to be.

So God sent Adam and Eve from the garden, but He sent them off with a memory of peace, a chance to begin again, a reason to change, and a new plan for their lives. He knew that in order to start over, they needed to be free from the past and live intensely in the present so that they could move beyond their consequences and shame into the freeing power of reconciliation and forgiveness that comes when one accepts the responsibility for one's actions. It is the same opportunity He gives you. It is a chance to know yourself better, and be better for knowing. I still wonder, though, what would have happened if, when discovered by God eating the forbidden fruit, Adam simply said, "I was wrong, I am sorry. Can we begin again?" I wonder what would happen if you simply said that same thing to someone you have offended, without any excuses.

# The Silent Treatment

I heard a story recently about a woman whose husband was dead for three days before she called for help. When the paramedics arrived, they asked her why she waited so long to call.

"I didn't realize he was dead," she said. "I thought he was just giving me the silent treatment."

I'm not sure if this is a true story or not, but the sad thing is, it could be. Anger isolates. No matter what spin is put on the inability to recognize, communicate, and deal with your emotions, it is foolhardy to ignore the evidence of what is really happening. I don't know what that woman did to incur her husband's anger. What I do know is that anger holds you hostage if you stay focused on the behavior of another rather than focus on your own feelings and how to deal with them. What a feat for that man to be so good at not communicating, at not reconciling, at not letting go of anger, that he could slip, unnoticed, into eternity. It's the kind of isolation experienced when you make external things central to the meaning of your life.

There is a time for anger, a time for calling us, and others, to accountability. But habitual anger is an enslaving traveling companion that seeks to destroy. The only difference between a rut and a grave is the depth. When you focus only on things outside your control, you lose control. Unless you learn to let go of a need to control the behavior of others, you will never be free of the anger that controls you. In some relationships, there is a need on the part of one person to blame the other for the anger felt, and an equal need by the other to accept that blame and to try to change to conform to the expectation of the other person. When you become comfortable in an environment of emotional dishonesty in order to survive in a relationship, you give up who you are. You give up the person God intends you to be. Your life is about more than just surviving a relationship with another person. Your life is about the inner conversion that transforms you by your relationship with God. If the admission price to a relationship with another person is to deny who you are and give up who God intends you to be, then the price is too high.

Faith is grounded, not in laws, but in a God who loves us, unconditionally. God's unconditional acceptance of who I am does not imply approval of all I do. It is a promise of love, and the encouragement of growth. When you have the courage to begin the process of letting go of anger, you find that you become less judgmental of the behavior of others. You also become more forgiving of your own behavior and of yourself. You let go of the need to be perfect and to expect perfection in others. You come to the realization that it is only with God, through God, and in God that we are perfected.

You cannot make another person like you. You can only let go of a need to be liked by that other person. Handing yourself over to the control of another does not guarantee your happiness. It only guarantees control. All spirits are entitled to be free. The only approval, acceptance, or appreciation you need is found in the view from the cross. It is a transforming relationship

*Unless you learn to let go of a need to control the behavior of others, you will never be free of the anger that controls you.*

with Christ that frees you of your anger toward others and your condemnation of their behavior. The ultimate freedom is realized only when you place your life in God's hands and give anger the silent treatment.

# The Suitcase

With less than an hour to spare, I raced into the airport only to find myself at the end of one of those really long lines, the kind that snakes around the ropes and out the door. I wished I had heeded the biblical advice of taking nothing for the journey. I pushed my suitcase along as I inched my way to the counter. I watched the others in line. Some struggled to move all their baggage even a foot at a time. Others clutched the handle of their bag as if it would run away if left on its own. Some counted their bags with each move forward. One person actually opened her bag twice to rearrange the contents. The truth is that however guarded the contents of our suitcases, we would eventually have to let them go in order to get on the plane and continue our journey.

Just to pass the time, I mentally unpacked my suitcase, taking everything out, except for what I really needed. I considered and reconsidered each item for its possible impact on my trip. I realized, by the time I got to the counter, that I could have taken nothing for the journey. Not only could I survive without the contents of my suitcase, but its weight was a burden that actually slowed me down. I came to the conclusion that everything I really needed I carried in my hand, my head, or my heart.

There are too many times life's journey is spent packing suitcases, traveling with layers of the past, hidden from view, weighing you down. The joy, the good times, the laughter, and the love travel light in your hearts. It is the pain that is packed into your suitcase that weighs you down. It is the lost dreams, the betrayed beliefs, the broken relationships, the wrongs done, the wounds that tore at the fiber of your being that often fill the baggage you carry. Perhaps you have learned to guard the suitcase and check on it often. The contents become so much a part of you that you begin to live out of your suitcase. What it holds defines the present and shapes the future. You pack, repack, and rearrange your suitcase. You own it, and it owns you. The truth is that you can never become the person you were meant to be if you continue to be the person you were when you packed your bags with pain, grudges, and disillusionment. You can never travel light if you continue to be burdened by the weight of a suitcase filled with wounds, real or perceived. Try as you might, you can't even unpack it without putting on the mantle of long-suffering that you have worn like a comfortable robe. Maybe it would be better if you would just lose your luggage. Losing that kind of luggage can be a blessing.

> *The truth is that you can never become the person you were meant to be if you continue to be the person you were when you packed your bags with pain, grudges, and disillusionment.*

Many years ago, my aunt's dog, a faithful companion for seventeen years, died. She called the animal shelter and asked if they could assist her in having the dog buried since she lived in the city in an apartment. She was told they would take care of it for her, but that she would have to bring the dog's body to the shelter since they had no one to pick it up. Since my aunt did not drive and never wanted to be a bother to anyone, she decided to put the dog in an old suitcase and take him to the animal shelter herself. She lovingly wrapped the dog's body in a blanket, put it in the suitcase, and headed for the subway. As she waited on the platform for the train, she clutched the suitcase to her, as if protecting her pain. A young man approached her and asked if he could carry her bag since it seemed to be weighing her down. She declined his offer. He insisted. Again she declined, holding the bag closer to her. Suddenly, the young man grabbed the suitcase from her hands and ran. My aunt started to cry out after the thief as he ran up the stairs, suitcase in hand, towards the crowded street above. She stopped and just watched him go. Her burden was lifted. Now, it was his. She shrugged her shoulders and headed for home, marveling at how God provides.

Maybe we can't all be unburdened as swiftly as my aunt. However, if what you are carrying in your suitcase that causes you pain is over, is no longer real, is in the past, then maybe you just need to let it go. Then you can shrug your shoulders and consider heading for home along the lightly traveled path of forgiveness, reconciliation, and love. Unburdened of your suitcase, you will no longer focus on your wounds or on those who wounded you. You will no longer focus on the hurt they caused. Instead, you can focus on the journey ahead, the journey of healing, and the journey of the heart. It is a journey you will travel, unencumbered, to a new beginning. If the dog in your suitcase is dead, then bury it, or let it go.

# Waiting in Line

There I was, running late and ready to make my purchase. There they were, long lines at the check-out counters ready to try my patience. It is almost predictable. Hurry up and wait. I got on the equally lengthy express line (10 items or less) and passed the time by counting the number of items in the baskets of the customers ahead of me. Do a dozen eggs count as one item or twelve? Then, something more interesting caught my attention. As if led by an internal rhythm, it happened—a line dance. Baskets scurried and darted from one line to another in search of the fastest checker, or the fastest moving line, as if there were a prize being given to the first customer out of the store. By the expression on the face of one "dancing" customer, I sensed that he believed that all the people in front of him had gotten up that morning with a common goal, to make him wait. All his sighing and glaring did nothing but make matters worse for him.

We live in a society where we really don't want to wait. We want what we want when we want it! The landscape is littered with reinforcements of our impatience: instant pain relief, instant foods, credit cards, fast service, drive-though windows, instant messages, stores that are open 24 hours a day seven days a week, an Internet that takes us anywhere, anytime, and e-mails that assume an immediate response. So whatever happened to waiting? How does waiting change things? Since we have learned how to manipulate the circumstances to get what we want now, why wait? We even expect God to conform to our impatience. We expect His "Yes." We will try to live with His "No." We refuse to accept His "Wait." So what ever happened to waiting?

Job waited in suffering. Joseph waited in prison. Zachariah waited in silence. They all prayed for deliverance from what they did not understand. God's answer was not "Yes" or "No." The answer was "Wait." Wait for God's time and see what happens.

If John the Baptist had been born years earlier as his parents wanted, his unique role would not have been fulfilled. Perhaps if you get what you want when you want it, it will keep you from getting something better if you wait. Manipulating the circumstances only causes the pain of relearning the same lessons over again. Looking beyond your hurt, your impatience, or your needs, and seeing what God is doing in your life through these circumstances, is what waiting is all about. Your unwillingness to wait for God's time limits your potential, and you may never become the person you were meant to be. Sometimes, in your impatience, you get desperate and do something foolish, just so that you can have it your way. Sometimes you are just not ready, and God knows it. Sometimes you just don't trust in the work of the Holy Spirit to transform your life into a new, improved creation. Even when you are filled with zeal about something new, sometimes it is just not the right time. So, what do you do when you think you are ready and circumstances keep you from getting started?

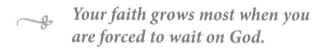

*Your faith grows most when you are forced to wait on God.*

After three years of teaching and an extra forty days following His Resurrection, Jesus had one final word of advice: "Wait!" (Acts 1:1). Sit down and wait for the gifts that reward your patience. These are the gifts of the Holy Spirit. He told it like it is. "It is not for you to know the times or seasons that the Father has established by his own authority" (Acts 1:7).

Your faith grows most when you are forced to wait on God. Your patience in waiting grows when you are forced to practice it. Sometimes you can practice patience just by waiting in line. Who knows whom you might meet, or what you might learn, while you are waiting? God does.

# Working Miracles

I saw an interesting infomercial on TV the other day for a piece of exercise equipment. I knew it must be a major breakthrough by the effortless way in which the announcer could work every muscle without sounding the least bit out of breath, as he raved about the miraculous results that anyone purchasing this equipment would experience. How effortless it all seemed. That was certainly the piece for me. I was tempted, until reality crept in. That piece would only serve to keep my treadmill residing upstairs from dying of loneliness. I have learned that to receive any benefit at all, I would actually have to get on the treadmill and do something. The benefits the announcer claimed sounded more like a miracle than work. After all, we live in a world that tells you the solutions to your problems are found outside yourself. If you have difficulties at all, it is because you haven't found the right program or product yet. You are not responsible for anything more than patience as you wait for miraculous results.

Oh, have no doubt, miracles do happen. I've seen more than a few. God does provide us with spontaneous enclaves of goodness in the midst of chaos. They occur most frequently as God's response to someone's actions of self-discipline, generosity, courage, and prayer. There is a story I heard that speaks to that response.

There once was a King who agonized over the tragedy, the poverty, and the violence in his kingdom.

He prayed to God, "Lord, my followers and I want to transform the kingdom. Is there anyway you could assist us?"

God replied, "Yes, would you like me to do it the miraculous way or the ordinary way?"

Not wanting to appear greedy the King replied, "The ordinary way."

At that very second, God sent legions of angels across the land in response to the King's request. Wars ceased, crops grew, and there was so much abundance that everyone worked and prospered. There was peace throughout the land.

The king was astonished and said, "Lord, if that was the ordinary way, what is the miraculous way?"

"If you would do it yourself," God answered.

God wants you to participate in the miracles of transformation. His miracles came with a call to action first: "Fill the jugs with water," "Collect the loaves and fish," "Take up your bed and walk."

He still calls you to action. There may be times when a person feels like that King. There may be times when you think there is nothing you can do. The problems seem overwhelming and without solution. There are times when you may think that confronting the chaos, complexity, and struggles in life will take nothing short of a miracle. At such times as these, how will you maintain your internal resolve and resiliency? The search for insight and transformation is a heroic journey, and the treasure at the end is worth the quest.

What is the miracle you are waiting for in your life? What is it you are willing to do to ensure peace, justice, or transformation, when fear continuously trickles into the flow of your thoughts? If it took a while for circumstances in your life, or the life of your family, to take a downward spiral, then it will take some time to change, and it is never too late. That kind of transformation begins in prayer, in patience, and in action. As Mark Twain said, "You can't break a bad habit by throwing it out the window. You have to walk it slowly down the stairs."

You have to take action first, and be patient with your progress. Within the vision that drives your actions, lie the seeds of a miracle, a miracle worth working for.

As for my interest in that latest physical fitness equipment, if I'm still looking for a miracle, perhaps the miracle will be that I actually go upstairs and give the treadmill a workout. Miracles do happen.

# The Devil's Pots

There is a Roman proverb that the Devil invented pots, but he didn't invent lids. How true! No matter what the "Old Boy" is cooking up, he can't keep a lid on it. It doesn't matter who his pot stirrers are, sooner or later his stewpot of chaos, wickedness, and all sorts of destructive behaviors will be revealed. Sooner or later it will bubble up, boil over, and the truth will be seen. Sometimes what's in the Devil's pots is just simmering. And sometimes we find ourselves praying that God will turn up the heat!

I thought about one such pot as I scanned the magazine racks at the airport. Article after article addressed the growing concern about overt, or covert, peer abuse that is called bullying. This issue has found its way into the mainstream of human behavior in all areas of daily life. The light of truth is being shed on behaviors that deny the dignity and seek to destroy the spirit of another. Peer intimidation, whether physical or emotional, is a learned, destructive tactic. It is not surprising that it is becoming more prevalent when current reality TV shows often glorify negative alliance building and subterfuge. What will one person do to another in order to win? How will one person crush the spirit of another? We easily recognize the stereotypical playground bully who takes particular delight in pushing someone off the swing or knocking another into a locker at school. Often what we don't recognize as quickly is covert aggression. That's the type of clandestine behavior that turned Palm Sunday into Good Friday. It is the type of behavior that seeks to destroy goodness.

Alternative aggression happens when one person, usually motivated by jealously, a fear of rejection, or failure, targets an unsuspecting victim for nothing more than being a perceived ego threat. The thinking behind this behavior is that by putting someone else down, the emotional bully will raise his or her own status or secure a position in a group. When I was a teacher, I sometimes saw the way those who practice social cruelty seek to devour their prey. These behaviors, if ignored, continue throughout the bully's life. The only difference is that with age, the bully gets better at the subtleness of relational aggression.

An emotional bully's power lies in the ability to maintain a façade of innocence, even persecution or injustice, while manipulating the consensus among a group of often unwitting co-conspirators. This type of bully never operates alone, but hides in a group, seeking the support of those who will often do the "dirty work." Meanness is justified. The alternative aggression that attacks another's self esteem or status, such as negative alliance building, the "silent treatment," isolation, rumors, or gossip, persists unquestioned. For the victim who is being shut out by a group, there are feelings of helplessness and doubt.

The victim begins to question what he or she could have done to cause this negative behavior in others. If adults have a difficult time dealing with covert aggression in the marketplaces of their lives, how are children expected to deal with it in the classrooms and playgrounds of their lives? It is a question that parents and teachers must pro-actively address together. How much longer should this behavior be tolerated, be seen as a rite of passage, or accepted as the way things are? Healthy people don't torture others; tortured people torture others.

 *Only God knows the duration and intensity of our trials, and only God's grace will give us the courage we need to withstand them.*

I remember one day after school, a bright, attractive, talented young girl sat in my classroom fighting back tears as she tried to figure out what she had done to cause a team she was on at school to turn so cruelly against her. She told me about her experiences that fluctuated between isolation by the team, to being invited to a sleepover only to be ridiculed and maligned by the group. My heart ached for her. I asked her, "Why would you want to be on a team that treats people the way you are being treated?"

She lowered her eyes and whispered, "What else can I do? I always wanted to be a cheerleader."

How could I help her? I realized that none of her friends on the team were secure enough to speak out in her defense for fear that if they did, they might be the next victims. A bully understands the power of a conspiracy of silence. What could I say to help her recognize that she did nothing wrong? She was negatively affected by the social problems of another. What could I do to help her become more resilient?

Experience taught me that these behaviors are not confined to any one place or group of people. What could I say to her to help her recognize that what seemed to her to be abandonment by her friends, was actually emotional abuse at the hands of a ringleader who was jockeying for a position of control? What did she need to hear from me to be able to speak the truth and discover the exhilarating freedom of honesty? How can a parent or a teacher keep a child from falling into that black hole?

This student took the first step: she sought help. Listen to your children and be aware of their relationships. Give them opportunities to develop many interests and meet many people. Help them express what it is they are feeling. We must name the behaviors that are eating away at the emotional well-being of our children, recognize them for what they are, and participate in eliminating them. Only God knows the duration and intensity of our trials, and only God's grace will give us the courage we need to withstand them. Use His grace to continue to shed the light of truth on all that robs us, or our children, of His peace. And, keep the lids off the Devil's pots.

# A History with GOD

# In the journey home

# The Beginning

It is said that there will come a time when you will think that everything has ended, and that will be the beginning. Not long ago, I thought that, for me, everything had ended. Several weeks ago, I had a stroke. It was never on my "to do" list, not part of my plan. It just happened. My first memory of that morning was hearing my husband, Joe, ask if I was getting up. I opened my eyes and responded. The response was only in my thoughts. I could tell by the look on his face that something was wrong. I couldn't understand why he didn't hear me, why I couldn't get up, and why he was calling 911. Try as I might, I could not speak, and I could not move my right side. I was trapped inside my own body. There was a disconnect between my mind and my physical reality. I ached for connectedness, but something was missing in the uncertainty of what lay beyond this time and place.

It was morning rush hour as the ambulance raced to the hospital. How many times have I pulled over as one rushed by, wondering what happened to the person inside and whispering a prayer? Now, it was my turn to ride in the back of the ambulance. I quickly learned that no matter how you get there, the back of an ambulance is a very lonely place. My thoughts turned to God. "Now what?" I asked Him. "Now what do You want from me?" At that moment it was God who broke through my weakened condition. I was in awe at the overwhelming sense of His presence. It was as if He sat down next to me. And, in my heart, I heard Him answer, "Everything." It didn't seem as if there was much left to give. In my heart I answered, "Take it, and hold on tight." At that moment, the fear of the unknown, the loss of control, was replaced by the acceptance of total dependency and the assurance of peace.

My past and my future converged in the emergency room. It was a strange feeling for an educator to not to be able to communicate, or to direct the activities around me. My family rushed to be with me. They talked to me, quizzed me, and reminded me of their love and all I had to fight for, especially my grandchildren. In spite of what everyone else saw, they recognized the person within. They held hands with me and prayed. It was in that oneness of our shared memory and our shared hope, that God returned to me my sense of connectedness to others.

Although I could not speak, I could hear and I could think. I heard the doctors tell my family that recovery was possible, but could mean quite lengthy therapy. I thought, "I don't think so! Let God decide that." So I gave it to God, and He gave it to all those people who put me in their prayers—all of those people in churches, in schools, in workplaces, in prayer groups, in private, who did for me what I could not do for myself. Their prayers lifted me up and carried me to Jesus to be healed. These people helped me, just like the man in the Bible whose friends helped him by lifting up his stretcher and lowering it through the roof of the house where Jesus was staying so that he could be healed. All of those people who prayed for me got Jesus' attention. They pointed me out to Him and asked Him to heal me. They will forever live in my heart and in my prayers. On my fourth day in the hospital, the doctor commented that he had no explanation for the rapid recovery I was experiencing. "I do," I responded. "It's prayer."

I continued to recover, and within weeks, returned to my family and to my work. I continue rejoicing in being a wife, a mother, a grandmother, a friend, and an educator. I have returned to the work I love as Superintendent of Catholic Schools, to speaking, to writing, and visiting the schoolchildren. The stroke is now a part of my history. Through God's grace, it will help me to become the person I was created to be, to accomplish what might not have been accomplished without it. What the world may view as harmful, God intends for good. This experience has helped conform me to His image and grow in His spirit of courage and faithfulness to His will, His plan.

My experience is not unique. There are those times when you too, each in your own way, find yourselves in a perilous place of loss or fear or woundedness. In these sorrowful times, it is not about what you want, what others say, the size of your

> *What the world may view as harmful, God intends for good.*

need, or your worthiness. It is about God. In these lonely times, no matter how well prepared you think you are, you should not try to rely only on your own strength, but rush quickly to God, knowing that only Jesus heals and only He decides how. No matter what rages against you, if you give it to God, He will take it and hold on tight to you. If you can't get to Him by yourself, trust Him to provide others, who through their prayers will lift you up and carry you to Him. I know this to be true. Not long ago I thought that, for me, everything had ended. I know now that it was the beginning.

# *Ghost Dancing*

Ghost Dancing originated in the late 1880's. It was a ceremonial religious dance practiced by several tribes of Native Americans who believed that the Ghost Dance would bring back their way of life, resurrect their customs and their culture. The tribes faced losing their freedom, their homes, their beliefs, in fact, their very existence to the civilization of the White Man that was being forced upon them. The Ghost Dancers danced to bring back the past. They believed the salvation of their future was not in a new creation, but in the restoration of the simplicity and happiness of the way things used to be in the past. They believed that the more they danced, the more the Great Father in the Sky would roll back the earth, covering the White Men and all their works, and the earth would be just as it was before the White Man came. It didn't happen, and the movement died out at Wounded Knee. There are times when I feel great empathy with the Ghost Dancers.

Have you ever been at a point in your life when you feel as if everything were over, that you had nothing left to give, nothing to do? Have you ever felt devastated by the loss of a spouse, a child, a friend, a job, your home or belongings? Have you ever been in that place where the circumstances of the present were so painful and difficult to accept because they changed everything you know, everything you have, everything you believe, and everything you have grown comfortable being? It is a place, like the Ghost Dancers experienced, when our faith is in our past and our hope lies in resurrecting that past for our future. There is no faith in the present, and that lack of faith affects our attitude and how we act in the now. We find it difficult to believe that things will ever work out. Our lives seem to be subjected to an alien domination of fear and uncertainty that is changing everything we know. It is in these times that we could be tempted to become Ghost Dancers. We might not ask for the earth to be rolled back, but we ask for time to be rolled back, back before our present circumstances, so that our lives would not change and everything would be like it was in the past.

If, in the present, you have come to a point where you think that everything is over, then that will be the beginning. The present belongs to God. It is in the pain of that void that God calls us to new life, a new beginning, a new dimension of our existence. Regardless of the feeling of long-suffering, the temptation to just give up, or to not see beyond the present circumstances, God is still at work in our lives. Without patience, without faith that God is in the present, His work in us will not be accomplished. We will miss what He is planning, what He is building in our lives. Don't make the present the spot in your life where you stop believing.

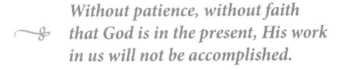

*Without patience, without faith that God is in the present, His work in us will not be accomplished.*

Know that God is in the present. He is in the sadness, in the loss, in the rejection, in the changes, even in our doubt that things will ever work out. It is His promise—"I know well the plans I have in mind for you...plans to give you a future full of hope" (Jeremiah 29:11)—that strengthens us and makes us more determined to trust Him to work in our present, to make the future even better than the past. Don't let the despair of a present situation project the nostalgia of the past into the future. Don't spend the present Ghost Dancing. Instead, take the hand that life deals you, whatever it might be, and win with it, by trusting God in the present.

# An Adventure in Love

It was a crazy idea, I know, but we did it anyway. My 97-year-old mother and I had a great adventure. We took a cruise together, just the two of us. Coming from a large family, it was actually the first time we had ever had the opportunity to spend that much time by ourselves. My parents loved to travel, and being believers in delayed gratification (their philosophy was pray, study, work hard, and relax, in that order), it wasn't until after their children were raised and on their own that they set out to see the world. They loved visiting other places and always told fascinating stories of their adventures. After sixty-seven years of marriage, my father died, and, after a lifetime together, he took his final trip without her. My mother continued to live her life as an example for the rest of us. Being confined to a wheelchair and not really able to care for herself, she thought her travels had come to an end. When I called to ask her if she wanted to go on a cruise with me, she jumped at the opportunity to be adventurous again. The trip became the focus of her thoughts and planning. So, when our departure day arrived, my brother drove us to the dock, a short ride from her home near Philadelphia, and we set sail for a week on the high seas traveling to Bermuda.

We didn't miss a thing during the cruise: the shows, the food (she ate things they could never serve in the nursing home where she lived), the people we met, and the things we did. We even went to the spa for a demonstration on how to combat the signs of aging. They were mildly surprised at my attendance, but when my mother wheeled in on her scooter, they looked stunned. We purchased the cream that they guaranteed would make anyone look ten years younger, and I told her that night at dinner it worked. She did not look a day over 87. The scooter made it easier for me than pushing a wheel chair, but it was a challenge for anyone, or anything, that got in her way. I would walk in front of her, clearing a path as we went. However, at one point, I told her that if she rode over my feet one more time, the scooter was going overboard. She just laughed and said, "Well, move your feet." But it was the routine we established that was the heart of the cruise. We would spend each morning on our balcony saying our prayers, reciting a rosary, eating breakfast, and talking for hours. Sometimes we were just two women who loved the same man—her husband and my father—recalling the impact of his life. And sometimes she told me stories of her life as a child that gave me insight into her, and into the genes that I inherited. One particular story I wrote down as she told it to me.

My mother said, "One day, when I was about six, my father took me to visit some relatives I had never met before. They lived in Camden, NJ. It seemed like a long way from Philadelphia, where I lived. One of the younger boys, about my age, was riding a tricycle. Around and around the yard he rode. It looked like fun. I wanted to try doing that. Finally, tired of watching him, I got up, ran over and grabbed the handles of the tricycle and said, 'It's my turn now!' He got off immediately. I rode the trike from then until the end of the visit. I guess he was too afraid to get it back from me. When we got home, my father told my mother of the incident. He was very proud of how I asserted myself. My mother questioned my behavior, a little embarrassed about the lack of gentility of a little girl. It is interesting the difference between the way men and women think. I learned that day that sometimes you just have to stand up for yourself and recognize that when your turn comes, you have to take it, or forever sit watching. Live life, or observe it being lived. Those are the only choices we really have."

I have thought about that story and how universal it really is. They are the same choices for all of us. It seems that the choice to get involved in life and the path you take in that choice speak of seeking your purpose in life, of discovering the plan God has for you. Sometimes you might feel as if you are just sitting and waiting for things to happen. Sometimes you might feel as if now is the time to act. What frees you to act is knowing that you don't have to worry about what it is, you just have to seize the opportunity to do God's will, to do what He has put before you, to care for those around you, to confront the injustice you see or experience, to choose to participate in life. God takes care of the details and blesses you during the process, even when the process is difficult or overwhelming, and you

> *What frees you to act is knowing that you don't have to worry about what it is, you just have to seize the opportunity to do God's will, to do what He has put before you, to care for those around you, to confront the injustice you see or experience, to choose to participate in life.*

feel lost or confused. Regardless of what you do in life, now or in the future, when you seek to do God's will, it will always be for your good and His glory if it is done in love, trusting the outcome to Him.

My mother, Mary Crowley, died the following January, just a few days shy of her ninety-eighth birthday. She was a kind and gentle woman whose love was without limits, and she saw the face of God in everyone she met. While I greatly miss her, I know that she and my father are rejoined for all eternity in the loving presence of God. I will always be grateful, crazy as it was, that we both seized the opportunity God put before us to learn more lessons and to live life together one last time.

# Something Is Missing

There is a world beyond our comprehension where reason steps back and the heart takes over. It is a world where wonder and wisdom meet. It is a world of faith. Annie and Jack are twins. They are my grandchildren. They were born five weeks earlier than expected. Each weighed a little more than four pounds. Annie was fine, but Jack had some problems. Jack was taken to the intensive care unit, Annie to her mother's arms. Annie went home. Jack stayed in the hospital. Annie didn't sleep well, and Jack didn't eat. He lost weight. When I visited him he seemed restless and I always asked him, "Do you miss Annie?" He would sleep with his arm wrapped around the tiny splint holding his feeding tube.

Several days passed and all Jack's other vital signs were now normal, but he still wasn't eating well or gaining weight. The doctors decided to send him home. They thought that perhaps being reunited with Annie would help. So Jack came home. My son laid him in the infant seat next to Annie. They seemed to sense each other's presence immediately. Annie stopped crying and nestled her head on Jack's shoulder. Jack leaned his head next to her head as if to say, "I missed you." They slept, peacefully. It was as if what they needed most was each other. There had been a piece missing from each of their hearts, shaped in the likeness of the other. Now, they were complete. Jack began eating, and Annie slept. They began thriving.

Jack and Annie's experience is really no different from our own when we sense that something is missing in our lives. There are times when you may feel empty or alone and you are not sure why. Perhaps you feel that something is missing in your life, in your work, in your relationships, or in your marriage. You might feel that there is something more that you need, but you don't know what it is. You look for every possibility to fill the void. Sometimes, you might fill that emptiness with what you think are solutions, such as a different job, a vacation, an affair, a bigger house, drugs, more stuff, more money, and on and on. You sometimes might even try to fill the void by blaming others for not meeting your need for fulfillment. You become so busy eliminating the possibilities of what it could be that is missing, that you often fail to see the simplicity of the truth. Our adult posturing prevents us from assuming a child-like faith. It is a faith that helps you recognize that there is indeed something more, and that "more" is God. What may be missing in the life you lead could be what is missing in you.

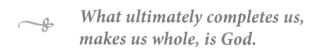 *What ultimately completes us, makes us whole, is God.*

What ultimately completes us, makes us whole, is God. There is a place in your hearts that only His presence can fill. And, when it does, there is no longer room for the restlessness, the need for more, for something else, that you might sometimes feel. You will have all you need to bring your whole self to whoever you are, and whatever you do. You can then be a complete presence for others. You will be content, you will thrive, and you will be at peace. Like Jack and Annie, you will still have your struggles. But now, you can rest peacefully and assured, knowing that you are not alone. You are always with God, who completes you, and you will sense His presence at your side.

# A Person of Influence

There is a passage from Walt Whitman's *Leaves of Grass* that reads, "A child goes forth each day, and the first object that the child sees, that object he becomes, for a day, or part of a day, or for days stretching into years." For me, as a child growing up, that "object" was my parents. What I saw in them, I have become, for days stretching into years. The older I get, the more it surprises me how much of me is them. A parent's influence never really stops. The influence really just transitions into the next roles as grandparent and great-grandparent, and lives on for generations. In fact, one's death notice should read, "…and is survived by ____, ____, and his influence." I wonder, however, if we are aware of just how strongly we influence our children, whatever the age of our children.

It is more than the mere external imitation, like the mini-mes we see at the Mall. We see fathers and sons wearing the same team shirts, or mothers and daughters dressed alike. It is an influence that internalizes attitudes and beliefs. It is an influence that has a sense of the spiritual, of following in one's footsteps, and of a willingness to learn. It is not just knowledge, but wisdom that is transmitted from person to person. Even if there are differences and rough roads and strains in the relationship along the way, for the most part, the influence outlasts any denial of it. And our children become us, just as we became our parents, for a day, or part of a day, or for days stretching into years.

In my own life, my parents' influence shaped my character, my values, and my faith. For them, it was not about settling for "as good as it gets." I identified with their example of continuous improvement, to be all you can be, all God calls you to be. The only person you have to be better than is the person you were yesterday. And they are still influencing me.

When my father, Joe Crowley, turned 95, we celebrated the event by having a book signing party for him. His first book, *Tales of a Landlocked Sailor,* had just been published. He started it a couple of years before when he was in the hospital for an extended stay. He said that "When an old person dies, a little bit of history dies with him." He wanted to share this little bit of history that he experienced with his grandchildren and great-grandchildren. It is not the story of his life, but rather remembrances of things that he had done or seen or heard over a long and eventful life. They are the kinds of things we just knew about each other in the days when people sat on front porches and talked.

His experiences span a time when more changes occurred than in any other period in history. Being a very private person, he never meant the stories to be read by anyone other than his family. But then they were published. After it was read by others, he learned that the book encouraged them to share their little piece of history, to sit on the front porch of the twenty-first century with their families and share their stories.

> *The footprints of Jesus whose invitation, "Come, follow Me," calls us to be a person of faith, a person of influence, a person who leads others to Him, for a day, or for days stretching into years.*

The book ends with a paragraph written to his grandchildren about the challenges they will face in their lifetime: "challenges to your values, challenges to your virtues, challenges to your way of life, challenges to your principles, challenges to your faith." But he is sure that "with your background and upbringing you will resist the temptations and overcome the challenges." In his own way, he is leaving footprints to follow. His work on a sequel stopped shortly after his birthday and the book signing party, when his condition worsened and he began Hospice care.

Leaving some work unfinished, but so much more completed, my father died on March 19, the feast of St. Joseph, for whom he was named.

In your own life, there is a child, a friend, a spouse, a coworker, or a relative who goes forth each day, and if the first "object" he or she encounters is you, what will he or she become because of you, for a day, or part of a day, or for days stretching into years? If you are to influence others to follow your footsteps, whose footsteps do you follow? If your plans for your own journey include continuous improvement, then there is only one set of footprints to follow. They are the footprints of Jesus whose invitation, "Come, follow Me," calls us to be a person of faith, a person of influence, a person who leads others to Him, for a day, or for days stretching into years.

# The Anniversary

When my parents celebrated their sixty-fifth wedding anniversary, my four brothers and I planned a weekend of surprises and celebrations for them. As I look back on it now, the most memorable times during the three days, for all of us, were the times we sat around telling "war stories" of who never got caught, who always got caught, who always got blamed, all time greats in the "Now you've done it" department, and who really threw the football through the picture window—twice. What seemed like disasters when they happened, have now become a source of humorous recollections at family gatherings. And my parents laughed the loudest. The experience reminded me of a Mark Twain saying: "My mother had a great deal of trouble with me, but I think she enjoyed it." I would like to think that from my children's perspective, I too, enjoyed parenthood.

Being a parent is never easy, but it is always an adventure. Just when my husband and I mastered one phase of our children's development, they moved into another phase. And, with each child, all the rules were rewritten. I never had the opportunity, or time, to develop a "been there, done that" attitude (except, perhaps, for changing diapers or hearing spelling words). And the adventures kept coming faster than we could keep up with the latest advice on parenting.

The only thing I can assure you, now that my children are adults, is that you are always a parent. Somewhere along the way it dawns on you that you have a lifetime job; there is no "bringing closure" to this assignment. And when you do realize this, you will be free to relax and enjoy the process. You will learn to make peace with the reality of "in progress" as a permanent state. When you learn that the bottom line is that there is no bottom line, then you will be able to find joy in a job that is not always enjoyable. No one ever said it would be easy, but no one ever said it couldn't be fun either. In spite of crises, illness, trials and tribulations, in a family, regardless of structure, is still the best place to be.

In his Gospel, John says, "There is no fear in love" (4:18). We should have no fear in parenting because parenting is love in action. Our fears come with our apprehensions, worries, and anxieties about the job we are doing. Fears come from our illusions that everything must be perfect or we have failed. They come from a society looking for scapegoats. If we wait for perfection, then we will never be free to love and enjoy doing what we do now. The active love of parenting helps us to move beyond ourselves to meet someone else's needs and follow the greatest command Jesus gave us: to love.

> *In spite of crises, illness, trials and tribulations, in a family, regardless of structure, is still the best place to be.*

Families aren't perfect, but in the "are we having fun yet?" test, it is more often than not, "yes." One of the greatest strengths a family has is to be able, when in the midst of sorrow, crisis, or bad times, to dwell on the good times. Families instinctively dig deep into their reserves of hope, trust, faith, patience, and love. I know, for me, dwelling on the good times with my family renewed my belief that the journey of parenthood has many rewarding and joyful stops. Of course, my parents still wanted to know who put the pin holes in the shape of the Big Dipper in their living room lamp shades—but we weren't talking.

# Begin With the End in Mind

It was sunny and warm, almost like an early Spring day, when I pulled out of my driveway. In spite of the weather, I knew that it was the day after Thanksgiving when I saw my neighbors arranging Christmas decorations on their lawns, hanging wreaths on their front doors, and tying bright red bows on their mailboxes. "It isn't Christmas Eve yet, I have plenty of time," I thought, as I glanced at my own lawn. I still had the four foot wooden witch that I put up for Halloween standing by my front door. The carved hat on the top of its head made it look more like a pilgrim than a witch, so I decided that it could span two decorating seasons and cover Thanksgiving as well. I made a mental note to put it away later. I didn't want to be three decorating seasons behind. As I drove down the street, I stopped for a minute to admire one of my favorite Christmas decorations. On a neighbor's front lawn stood a wooden manger filled with straw, a likeness of the makeshift cradle that held the infant Jesus at His birth. Behind it, at the head of the manger, stood a six foot wooden cross, a likeness of the one that held Jesus' body at his death. "Begin with the end in mind," I thought, "how appropriate." All the display needed was a depiction of the Resurrection, perhaps a huge boulder next to an empty tomb, and the message would be complete.

Begin with the end in mind. The thought was not just for Steven Covey's advice on the habits of highly effective people. After attending three funerals in the course of a week and a half, I was acutely aware of just how significant that thought is in the lives of all people, lives filled with joy and sorrow, love and loneliness, hope and despair. And, three times in that week and a half, I was very conscious of the little dash that comes between the dates of one's birth and death. That one little line represents all that was done, the life that was lived, and the impact of that life on the lives of others. That dash is who you are, all that comes between your birth and death. It is your ticket to heaven. How is it validated? How many times is it punched? Begin with the end in mind, like the Wise Men. Find God first, before you think you need Him. The manger and the cross depict a life that we are all called to live. You are here not just to be, but to become, knowing where you are headed.

*The manger and the cross are signs of the promise from God that binds us all to hope. Jesus is the center of that promise.*

The manger and the cross are signs of the promise from God that binds us all to hope. Jesus is the center of that promise. It is the promise that God is always with you, not just at the beginning or at the end, but throughout your life. He lives on that dash with you, in your joys and in your crosses. No matter how you start out in life, no matter your struggles, successes, trials, or blessings, God is the source and finish of it all. Sorrow and failure are worldly by-products of a life worth living when you choose actions that glorify God and lift up others; when you begin all you do with the end in mind. Beginning with the end in mind is knowing where you are headed, knowing that heaven is always before you. It is a promise of majesty in the mundane, divinity in the daily acts of faithfulness, and everlasting life in living out a faith that is hope beyond vision. It is living a life that takes up the cross of love with no strings attached. And when you do begin all things with the end in mind, you will know the fulfillment of God's promise of the manger, the cross, and the empty tomb.

# The Last Laugh

Grandparents are noted for the things they teach their grandchildren. When I was a little girl, my grandfather taught me how to draw horns, beards, and mustaches on people whose pictures were in the newspaper. With a twinkle in his eye, he told me it was always better to do this before anyone else read the paper. It would make it more interesting for anyone who read it. So we'd sit on the floor and get to work. I told him that I didn't think it would really make anyone as happy as he thought it would because the ink always covered up the words on the other side of the page. But he'd just laugh, and we'd do it anyway. He'd laugh a lot. When I was eight my grandfather became very ill. One morning we got a call that he had taken a turn for the worse. The family gathered around his bed: his wife, ten children, in-laws, and hoards of grandchildren. My Aunt Lillian, a Religious Sister, thought it would be a good idea to sprinkle my grandfather with holy water after we said the Rosary. She very ceremoniously waved the bottle in the direction of my grandfather. As she did, the top flew off and the entire contents of the bottle landed in my grandfather's face. He woke up, wiped the water from his face, and with a fading twinkle in his eyes said, "You don't have to drown me, Lilly, I'm going as fast as I can." Everyone laughed, and so did my grandfather. It was his last laugh.

There is an expression that says that he who laughs last, laughs best. I'm not sure who first said that, or how it started, but it seems to me to be a very good description of hope, of resurrection, of a final theology. Laughter is a gift that brings perspective. It is an invisible force made present by the determination to believe that God is good, that life is beautiful, and perseverance, in spite of your circumstances, is divine. It is no somber God who gave you such a gift. He knew you would need it. You need it whatever you do, wherever you are, however burdened you might be, to see you to the outcome God has waiting for you and to bask in the joy of His laughter.

There are hundreds of references throughout the Bible to suffering, sorrow, and death. Those found laughing are few, but they always seemed to be the ones having the last laugh. Job, in the midst of his misery, was told he would laugh in the face of evildoers, and eventually, he did. Proverbs says the wise will laugh and, according to the Psalms, it will be the righteous. Sarah laughed, too, at the absurdity of God's promise of a son in her old age (Genesis 18:22). But it was God who had the last laugh when the promise was fulfilled. Trying to control a present situation does not guarantee your success. Being controlled by others does not guarantee your happiness. One of the choicest consolations of the present, regardless of the circumstances, is that you are getting nearer to the last laugh when you give

*Laughter is a gift that brings perspective. It is an invisible force made present by the determination to believe that God is good, that life is beautiful, and perseverance, in spite of your circumstances, divine.*

the outcome to God. It is like an intimate joke between friends who know that their laughter is really about love. Having the last laugh emphasizes the one who has control in the end, even when others seem to have the advantage in the present. When you are burdened by the weight of the present circumstances, or the threat of evil, you will be able to endure much because you know that the last laugh really belongs to God, who is the source of our joy.

# The Gift

---&---

Sometimes the greatest gifts come disguised and humble, tucked inside plain brown envelopes. I know. I received one that came to me just that way. Shortly after my mother died, I was sorting through her mementos that had been tucked away in a box on a shelf in the back of her closet. They were just those small, personal remembrances that you put away for safekeeping because they have a special place in your heart. They are the reminders of what matters most to you. They are usually things with no real monetary value, but in sentimentality, they are priceless. As I looked in the box, I felt as if I were reading the postscript of the story of my mother's life that said, "These are the things that are always important."

Inside the box was a piece of lace from her wedding dress. It was a reminder of the day that she and my father began their marriage of sixty-seven years. She saw love, commitment, and patience in that piece of lace. There were five locks of baby curls, each tied with a ribbon, from her five children's first haircuts. To a mother, her children are always her children, no matter the age or the separation of time or place. There were no locks of her gray hair to which those five children undoubtedly contributed. There were pictures of Baptisms, First Communions, birthdays, four generations at Christmas, faded prayer cards given at the funerals of loved ones, and a large brown envelope. I opened the envelope and poured the contents onto the table. There, before me, lay a pile of cards that I had given to my mother years ago. Most of the cards, the ones given to her when I was a child, were handmade on sheets of plain white paper, folded to look like the cards I had seen at the store. The ones I made were decorated with flowers and hearts and stick figures, some drawn in pencil, some in crayons. Some were written in large, childish print, some in shaky first attempts at cursive writing. Some I even signed with my first and last name, just so she didn't confuse me with another Mary. The pictures I drew on the cards were of my mother, or the entire family, or religious scenes, celebrating a variety of events like birthdays and Christmas. My artistic ability definitely peaked at about fourth grade when the sick figures filled out a bit; however, they were still very generic-looking. I remembered that as I grew older I earned the money to buy the fancy cards at the store. The cards and the occasions for them varied, but the heading on each was the same, "A Spiritual Bouquet for You." I learned about Spiritual Bouquets, gifts of prayer, at school. Inside each card was listed the gifts that I had given to my mother for that special occasion as a token of love and gratitude, such as ten visits to the Blessed Sacrament, or fourteen Rosaries. On one card I had written "1,950 aspirations," those short little one-line prayers. I might still owe her a few of those.

> *It is the gift of prayers said by others on your behalf to sustain you, support you, strengthen you, console you, encourage and comfort you that lasts a lifetime.*

I sat there in awe. Of all the material gifts I had given her over the years, my mother saved these spiritual gifts, these gifts you couldn't see or touch or admire or wear. These gifts of prayer were worth remembering. It was her gift back to me. It was a reminder that what is really important in life is the spiritual gift we give each other. It is the gift of prayers said by others on your behalf to sustain you, support you, strengthen you, console you, encourage and comfort you that lasts a lifetime. You don't see the prayers, but you feel them, and you sense it when you are remembered in prayer. The time and experience you have while praying for others lift you as well as those for whom you pray.

Looking at the cards, I recalled the times in my life when others prayed for me, and how important it was to know that. There are times when you are too weak, too frightened, or too grief-stricken to pray for your own circumstances. It is at those times that you count on the prayers of others, those spiritual good Samaritans, to lift you up and carry you to Jesus to be healed. It is through their efforts that you get Jesus' attention. They point you out to Him when you can't do it for yourself. It is the spiritual gift of prayer, the prayers of an individual, a prayer group, or to have your name put on a list that requests the prayers of strangers for you, that defines the essence of gift-giving by lifting the soul of another.

As I carefully placed all the cards back in the envelope, I said a prayer for my mother, thanking her for the gift she just gave me. She reminded me that the time you spend in prayer on the behalf of another is a gift to them, and to you. It's a gift that keeps on giving.

# With God, All Things Are Possible

A nd the angel said to her, "Do not be afraid, Mary....For nothing will be impossible for God" (Luke 1:30, 37).

I have pondered those words often during those times in my life when I saw no way out of a crisis, no good ending in the midst of a storm. When a circumstance in my life seemed hopeless, I would wonder how God could bring something good from what I thought was an impossible situation. And yet, time after time, I saw His hand in an outcome I could have never imagined. There was just such a time in my life when God broke through and showed me, yet again, that with Him all things are possible.

It was just an ordinary day, filled with a few too many things to do. As I drove from one of our schools back to my office, I felt a sharp pain in my chest unlike anything I have ever experienced. I was just a few blocks from my house so I headed there and called my husband, Joe. By the time I pulled into my driveway, I knew I was sinking fast so I called 911 for help. The ambulance and my husband arrived at the same time. By then, my pulse was faint, and my blood pressure barely detectable. I drifted in and out of consciousnesses as I was rushed to the hospital. The emergency room was alive with purpose driven activity as the doctors and nurses tried to stabilize me. I was in extreme shock. The ordinary day was gone, and I was fighting for my life.

It was not known at the time that I was brought into the hospital that a small device implanted about a year before to close a hole in my heart had malfunctioned and perforated my aorta. I was bleeding to death internally. All I knew was that I was in a crisis, an impossible situation. Over and over in my mind I repeated the words, "Do not be afraid. With God all things are possible." It gave me peace and an overwhelming sense of acceptance of whatever was happening.

My conditioned worsened. Waves of intense agony came over me as my heart, drowning in blood, struggled to beat. My family had gathered around me. I looked at my son, Matt, and said, "I don't think I am going to make it. This must be what Christ felt on the cross." I cried out as the pain intensified, and then suddenly, I was silent. My eyes, open and fixed, saw nothing. While the doctors heroically worked on my body to save my life, I waited someplace else. It was a place beyond pain. It was a place that hovered between life and death. It was the reality of belief.

I have a vivid memory during this brief time of waking up in a place that was bathed in a crystal blue light. I felt an intense sense of peace, a peace beyond comprehension. I was home. There was no pain, no fear, and no sorrow. I felt free of everything that would burden me. I was overcome with a feeling of extreme love that I cannot begin to explain. I was not alone. I saw three translucent figures off to one side, and a fourth standing closer to me. They all smiled. The crystal blue light shown through them. The peace intensified. Then I heard voices call my name. It was a faint sound at first. I ignored it as I clung to what I was experiencing. The voices grew louder. "Mary, come back. Stay with us, Mary, stay with us." I knew that if I went to where they were it would be painful, but I felt drawn to their pleas. I looked at the figures as they drew near and said, "I'm sorry. I have to go. They need me." The beautiful figures smiled. In an instant the soft blue light became a bright white light. My eyes moved. I saw the doctors standing over me and felt an intense wave of pain. I knew I was alive. I saw my family in the hall as I was wheeled to the operating room for emergency open chest surgery to repair my aorta. I called to them, "I love you. Ask people to pray." They prayed, and I am here.

Since my near-death experience, I realize in a new way what it means to be born into eternal life, to rest in peace. The promises of Christ are fulfilled in death. I realize in a new way that your life on earth is temporary, that you are on a journey to a place where the only thing you take with you is who you are. God is always with you on your life's journey, whether you realize it or not. Death itself, whether painful or peaceful, is also a journey and you are never alone. God journeys with you in death, as He does in life, and He sends His angels to watch over you. I realize in a new way that the blessing of the gift of life is to live in such a way as to foreshadow an eternity of peace in the presence of God. No matter how difficult life is, no matter the pain, the fear,

> *We need not be afraid,*
> *for God is always with us.*

the sorrow, the struggles, there is comfort in knowing that there is a place where you will join with those who have gone before. It is a place of perfect love, of incomprehensible peace. It is the place promised to us by Jesus.

It was not the easiest lesson I ever learned, but surely the most profound. We need not be afraid, for God is always with us. And with God, all things are possible.

# More Than One Day

On a trip to the store just two days before Christmas, I noticed two clerks shifting all the candy canes, tree ornaments, and velvet poinsettias to one end of the seasonal display aisle. I overheard one of the clerks say, "Move that Christmas stuff down, and put those red heart candles on the shelf." It is no wonder that time seems to pass so quickly. We live in a society whose watch ticks by card-sending occasions heralded weeks before the event arrives. Even before the last Christmas decoration is put away, the first barrage of red hearts appears, and the seasonal giving frenzy begins, again. Although Valentine's Day has become the Super Bowl of the outward display of affection, it pales in comparison to the inner force of a love that is quietly lived out day by day, noticed only by those whose lives it affects. The expression of love is about more than one day.

"For God so loved the world that he gave his only Son" (John 3:16). "No one has greater love than this, to lay down one's life for one's friends" (John 15:13). "Love is patient, love is kind" (1 Corinthians 13:4).

Love is not just a feeling. Love is an action throughout the Bible. God speaks to us of the incredible power of love. Love is God's life in us and lived out through our service to Him and others. Love is a power that overcomes hate and causes us to lift up one another. It helps us continually to reach a higher level. Love is faith and hope in action. Love is risking the difficult now for the good of the long haul. Love is doing the right thing, not just saying the right thing. Love is modeling the integrity, honesty, and character in ourselves that we want to develop in our children. Love is bringing out the best, even when we only see the worst. Love is not easy. The burden of fatigue rests on the shoulders of a parent, a spouse, a friend, from the patience needed to live that kind of love day after day.

What do I know of love?

I know that it is love that directs the character and shapes the lives of your children. I know that it is love that rocks crying babies and answers a thousand questions from an inquisitive child. I know that it is love that hears spelling words, over and over, and appreciates a homemade cake with a crack down the middle. I know that it is love that withstands an adolescent's insatiable need to be daring and different. It is love that wraps its heart around a wayward child, waiting and praying for his homecoming, no matter how long it takes. I know that it is love that reaches out to the lost and the lonely and the painfully shy. I know it is love that forgives, over and over again. I know that it is love that puts a smile on the face of a dying person. It is love that hung on the cross, and love that stood at the foot of it. It is love that makes a parent, not a person to lean on, but a person to make leaning unnecessary. Love is the only relationship theory that works, especially at those times when you feel that another person least deserves to be loved. Love is a decision. It does not come with "if" or "when" or "unless." It is unconditional. Love

> *Love is a decision. It does not come with "if" or "when" or "unless." It is unconditional.*

does not manipulate a relationship, but is committed to it. There are no strings attached, no fine print.

Where do we find this kind of love? It is certainly not on a seasonal display aisle. Look no farther than that which is already within you. When we empty our hearts of a self-generated love and fill them with the power of God's love, then His spirit flows through us and we become His response to the needs of others for love and acceptance. And the more love we give, the more we are filled up with a love that lasts more than one day. In the end there are only three gifts that last—faith, hope, and love. And the greatest of these is love.

# The Overnight Success

The label "Overnight Success" has been mistakenly used to describe someone whose achievement is actually the result of a lifetime of hard work, sacrifices, and making right choices. From everything I have heard or experienced, being an overnight success takes a long time, much longer than one night. It is true that the world may quickly become aware of someone's success, but the long, hard struggle that led to the achievement is the real success. Ask anyone who has won an Olympic medal, overcome an addiction, found a cure for a disease, or celebrated a fiftieth anniversary, if they just started their quest the day before. Success at anything is never as easy as it looks. Do you remember when you learned to tie your shoes, ride a bike, read? Did you give up because it took time and patience, or did you just keep working at it until you succeeded? We are all still working at something. The only difference is that the number and intensity of the things you struggle with now may require a lot more time, practice, prayer, and patience with yourself and others.

I guess it is patience, that quiet, persevering trust in the slow work of the Lord, that is the key to the success of the process of the transformation of from what you are, to what you can become, to be the person that God intends you to be. The most difficult lesson to learn just might be that it is never too late for any of us. The spiritual journey requires the toughest training and the most patience. Your pursuit of goodness will not be an overnight success. When you strive to "seek first the kingdom (of God)" (Matthew 6:33) it won't be easy. You can be sure of a lifetime of hard work, sacrifices, and making right choices. But the reward is eternal, and the success of others inspires you along the way.

When the going gets rough, look for those overnight successes, those ambassadors of hope, those spiritual role models who have been in similar situations, to inspire you to keep going, to try a little harder, a little longer. In my life I have learned from the example of everyone from famous saints to nameless sinners and good Samaritans. And all of them, with the possible exception of the Good Thief, took longer than overnight to succeed in the quest for the heavenly reward. Just ask St. Paul, St. Augustine, St. Monica, St. Peter, the woman at the well, or the prodigal son about how long the journey took. Delay does not mean disaster when you put your success in God's hands and not in decisions that involve only worldly success.

*Delay does not mean disaster when you put your success in God's hands, and not in decisions that involve only worldly success.*

So, when it comes to the only success that really counts, your eternal reward, you must commit yourself to a lifelong journey with Christ, struggles and all, that will be recognized in His welcome home to you: "Well done, good and faithful overnight success!"

# Waiting for God

The situation is desperate. There is no hope of rescue. Panic reigns in the crowded streets. Just then, the people point to the sky saying, "Look! Up in the sky! It's a bird. It's a plane. It's Superman!"

And Superman comes swooping in to save the day, right on time, which in the early days of TV was thirty minutes. That was the time allowed. It was the power of that universal hope of being rescued from a crisis that turned the story of a visitor from another planet who came to earth to fight for truth and justice, into a pop culture national hero, and left the impression that we deserved to be rescued without much more than a thirty minute wait. But the realities of life are a bit more complex, and waiting for Superman is not the same as waiting for God. I had the chance to think about that not long ago.

It's one of those questions that occasionally crosses my mind when I ride an elevator, or during that two-second delay before the doors open, "What would I do if this thing breaks down and I'm trapped in here?"

I got my answer. As I rode alone on an elevator from the top floor of a high-rise office building, I felt an unexpected jolt as the elevator stopped, and the doors remained closed. I waited. Nothing happened. The lights went out. I pressed the emergency button, and every other button as well. I waited. Nothing happened. I used my cell phone to call the office where the meeting I had just attended was held. They assured me that they would contact the management of the building and inform them of my plight. They kindly offered to stay on the phone until help arrived. I looked at the low battery indicator light on my phone and regretfully declined their offer. Time passed with no sign of help. After another call, I was informed that it would probably take a lot longer to determine exactly how to fix the problem. Where is Superman when I need him, I thought. I had done everything I could do to help myself. There was nothing I could do to change my situation. I had come to a point where the only thing left to do was wait. As I sat and waited, I began to think about three persons in my life whose waiting is still an inspiration to me.

I was living in Virginia Beach, Virginia, when the American prisoners of war were released from captivity in Viet Nam. Navy Captain Jeremiah Denton was a POW for seven years. I cannot even imagine what life was like for him and the other prisoners for those seven years. I remember talking to him after Mass the Sunday following his return home to Virginia Beach. Our parish had prayed for a miracle, and here he was, home safely. I looked into his eyes and saw the reflection of God's grace.

"How did you get through it?" I asked, looking for an insight into his courage.

"I prayed and waited for God's time. I never gave up hope," he responded.

He placed a horrific situation in God's hands and waited. Captain Denton was home. He went on to become an Admiral, and then a United States Senator from Alabama, all in God's time.

When I was a teacher, one of the students in my class mysteriously vanished from her home. An intruder had kidnapped her from her bedroom during the night. For four months her whereabouts, and the circumstances of her disappearance, were unknown to everyone but her and her captor. For all the rest, there were only rumors, false leads, searches, prayer vigils, police interviews, an empty bedroom, an empty desk, bouts of despair, and flashes of hope. For four months, she was held captive in the attic of a church just a few miles from her home and a few blocks from her school. Then, as unexpectedly as she had disappeared, she was found. She returned home to a family who never lost hope. I remember the day she returned to school, determined to resume her life where it was so cruelly interrupted. I looked into her eyes and saw the reflection of God's grace.

"Where did you find the strength?" I asked, looking for an insight into her perseverance.

"I prayed and waited for God's time," she responded. "I never gave up hope."

She placed an incomprehensible situation in God's hands and waited. She has gone on to become a successful attorney, a joyful wife and mother, all in God's time.

Several years ago, my dear friends' son, John, was diagnosed with Leukemia. During the months following his diagnosis, John was a patient at St. Jude's Children's Hospital. His treatments left the adolescent athlete weakened and virtually helpless to do anything but wait: wait for the latest medical update, wait for the new protocol to take effect, wait for his life to resume, wait to feel even a little bit better. I sat with John on one of the rare occasions his parents left his side. I remember our conversation. I looked into his eyes and saw God's grace reflected there.

"How are you handling this?" I asked, looking for an insight into his determination.

"I pray and wait for God's time," he responded.

It was a response I had heard before. He placed what appeared to be an insurmountable situation in God's hands and waited. John is in remission now. He has gone on to graduate from college, pursue a successful career, and is a husband and father, all in God's time.

*Place your situation in God's hands. He is already in the process of saving the day. You must be in the process of trusting, praying, and waiting in hope for God's time.*

Perhaps a time will come when you will find yourself in a situation that seems hopeless. Nothing you do, or could ever do, can change your seemingly insurmountable circumstances. You may feel a sense of helplessness as you become more and more dependent on the actions and decisions of others. You may wonder if anyone even understands your fears as you reach for even the smallest thread of hope. How will you get through it, the hours, days, or even years of uncertainty, of fear, of waiting? Who will come to save the day? There is only one answer. It is so simple, yet often so difficult to do. Place your situation in God's hands. He is already in the process of saving the day. You must be in the process of trusting, praying, and waiting in hope for God's time.

"Are you okay in there?"

"We'll have you out shortly."

"Shortly" was much longer than expected, but finally the elevator doors opened. My waiting was over. But the waiting turned out not to be the crisis I envisioned. The waiting was a gift. It was a valuable experience of the wisdom of doing nothing more than trusting, praying, and waiting for God's time.

# About the Author

 Mary Crowley McDonald, Ed.D., has served as the Superintendent of Catholic Schools for the Diocese of Memphis (West Tennessee) since 1998. Prior to that, she served as Principal of St. Benedict at Auburndale (PreK-12th grade) and Principal of St. Agnes Academy elementary. McDonald has taught at the elementary, high school, and university levels. She has been involved in Catholic education since 1966 when she began her teaching career as a math teacher at St. Maria Goretti High School in Philadelphia.

As Superintendent of Schools for the Diocese of Memphis, McDonald's responsibilities include oversight for all aspects of the system of Catholic schools in the Diocese of Memphis, as well as for the creation of the Jubilee Catholic Schools, eight long-closed Catholic schools that were reopened in the inner city of Memphis. As the architect of the Jubilee Schools, she developed the infrastructure, professional management system and governance model, and is responsible for ongoing oversight, funding, and accountability for the schools.

McDonald is very involved in the community, locally as well as nationally. She is an advisor to the Education Committee of the United States Conference of Catholic Bishops (USCCB), a graduate of Leadership Memphis, and the Regional Representative for the National Catholic Educational Association (NCEA). She has served on the University of Notre Dame's Task Force for Catholic Education and the National Catholic Educational Association Strategic Planning Task Force. She is currently Secretary of the National Black Catholic Congress Education Board. She has been involved with Gateway Technology Inc. (National Advisory Board Member), Rotary Club of Memphis (Board Member), Facing History and Ourselves (Advisory Board Member), Diversity Memphis (Board President), Serra Club of Memphis (Past President), Shelby County Regional Health Council, The Society of Entrepreneurs, and is a member of the Equestrian Order of the Holy Sepulcher.

McDonald was a recipient of the Humanitarian of the Year Award given by the National Council for Community and Justice. She has been recognized by the University of Notre Dame, receiving The Notre Dame Exemplar Award for Outstanding Contributions to Education, Christian Brothers University, receiving the Carroll T. Dozier Humanitarian Award for Peace and Justice, Facing History and Ourselves for Making a Positive Difference in the Community, Knights of Peter Claver Humanitarian Award, Kappa Delta Pi Award for Outstanding Contributions to Education, Immaculata College Amethyst Award for outstanding contributions in community service and education, the UNICO Humanitarian of the Year Award, the Immaculata Medal for Creative Leadership and Sound Scholarship, and The University of St. Thomas Humanitarian Award. McDonald leads by example and works to make education a vehicle for understanding diversity, promoting unity, and making the future brighter for all children.

An accomplished author, McDonald's first book, *A Light Reflected,* was published in 2003. She writes a regular column for the *West Tennessee Catholic Newspaper*. She is also published in other local and national publications. McDonald gives workshops and is a consultant in numerous areas of education, including teacher effectiveness and student achievement, leadership and governance, faculty and staff development, parenting, urban education, and various other topics at the local and national levels. She and her husband, Joe, have two adult children and six grandchildren.

# Also available from the
# Alliance for Catholic Education Press

**No Greater Work: Meditations on Church Documents for Educators**
Edited by James M. Frabutt,
Anthony C. Holter, & Ronald J. Nuzzi

ISBN 978-1-935788-01-0
5.5 x 8.5 paperback / 204 pages

List Price: **$12.00**

*Prayers to Guide Teaching*
by Gail Mayotte, SASV

ISBN 978-0-9788793-2-7
6 x 9 paperback / 58 pages

List Price: **$6.00**

For ordering information,
visit the Alliance for Catholic Education Press website:
**http://acepress.nd.edu**

CPSIA information can be obtained
at www.ICGtesting.com
Printed in the USA
273952LV00001B